# W. B. YEATS AND THE CRAFT OF VERSE

Malati Ramratnam

UNIVERSITY PRESS OF AMERICA

LANHAM • NEW YORK • LONDON

4720 Boston Way
Lanham, MD 20706

3 Henrietta Street
London WC2E 8LU England



Printed in the United States of America

**Library of Congress Cataloging in Publication Data**

Ramratnam, Malati, 1940-
W.B. Yeats and the craft of verse.

Revision of thesis (Ph. D.)—Brandeis University.
Bibliography: p.
Includes index.
1. Yeats, W. B. (William Butler), 1865-1939—Style.
2. Yeats, W. B. (William Butler), 1865-1939—Technique.
I. Title. II. Title: WB Yeats and the craft of verse.
PR5908.S8R36 1985 821'.8 85-20824
ISBN 0-8191-5017-7 (alk. paper)
ISBN 0-8191-5018-5 (pbk. : alk. paper)

All University Press of America books are produced on acid-free paper which exceeds the minimum standards set by the National Historical Publications and Records Commission.

*To*

*my father and mother*

# CONTENTS

# ILLUSTRATIONS

# PREFACE

THE CRITICISM of Yeats's poetry in general has been concerned with his capacity for mystic vision and thought. However, with this gift Yeats combines extraordinary deliberate labor in the making of his style. He often speaks of poetry as a craft requiring toil. This aspect of Yeats's work deserves fuller consideration than it has received. This book explores his craftsmanship and makes a new and necessary contribution to the criticism of his technique and its relation to his thought.

The first chapter deals with his theory of the poet as craftsman. The succeeding chapters consider Yeats at work on the making of his idiom, rhythmic structure, and the dramatic form of his poem.

This book is a revised version of my doctoral dissertation on Yeats's craftsmanship accepted by Brandeis University. I am grateful for the help I have received from Professor Allen R. Grossman of Brandeis.

M.R.

Weston, Massachusetts

'A line will take us hours maybe;
Yet if it does not seem a moment's thought,
Our stitching and unstitching has been naught.
Better go down upon your marrow-bones
And scrub a kitchen pavement, or break stones
Like an old pauper, in all kinds of weather;
For to articulate sweet sounds together
Is to work harder than all these, and yet
Be thought an idler by the noisy set
Of bankers, schoolmasters, and clergymen
The martyrs call the world.'

W.B. YEATS, 'Adam's Curse'

# CHAPTER I
# THE POET AS CRAFTSMAN

One of the qualities of Major Robert Gregory that Yeats admires is his fine connoisseurship of the arts and the crafts:

> What other could so well have counselled us
> In all lovely intricacies of a house
> As he that practised or that understood
> All work in metal or in wood,
> In moulded plaster or in carven stone?[1]

These lines of praise for Gregory could be applied to Yeats's own sensitivity to and interpretation of numerous arts and crafts in his work. Indeed this constant "descant upon the supreme theme of Art and Song"[2] in its relation to wisdom is one of the major preoccupations of Yeats. He laments that the world should have lost "the old nonchalance of the hand"[3] at work on art objects. He lingers wistfully on the recollections of the beautiful things that are now no more:

> Many ingenious lovely things are gone
> That seemed sheer miracle to the multitude,
> Protected from the circle of the moon
> That pitches common things about. There stood
> Amid the ornamental bronze and stone
> An ancient image made of olive wood—
> And gone are Phidias' famous ivories
> And all the golden grasshoppers and bees.[4]

This elegiac mood lamenting the passing of beautiful things—either violently destroyed or silently gone out of mind—expresses itself in numerous recollections of a dead or dying tradition of art;

phrases like "famous old upholsteries,"[5] "the abounding glittering jet"[6] in the garden, "the glory of escutcheoned doors,"[7] "peacocks upon old terraces,"[8] "old marble heads,"[9] "beloved books that famous hands have bound,"[10] are suggestive of this elegiac tone. In the midst of all this decaying beauty of art, some objects retain a relative permanence, and in their beauty, their unity of form and matter, and their perfection of skill become symbolic of the "artifice of eternity."[11] Sato's sword made before Chaucer was born becomes for him what the Grecian Urn was to Keats:

> The consecrated blade upon my knees
> Is Sato's ancient blade, still as it was,
> Still razor-keen, still like a looking-glass
> Unspotted by the centuries;
> That flowering, silken, old embroidery, torn
> From some court-lady's dress and round
> The wooden scabbard bound and wound,
> Can, tattered, still protect, faded adorn.[12]

If works of art become symbols of the permanence of being and tell dying generations of the oneness of truth and beauty, they can express more sweetly some old religious vision than words can:

> The true faith discovered was
> When painted panel, statuary,
> Glass-mosaic, window-glass,
> Amended what was told awry
> By some peasant gospeller.[13]

It is significant that Yeats in his finest poems exploring the nature of reality, or of the soul, or of the unity of body and soul should turn to the arts for his symbols and his philosophy. 'Leda and the Swan,' 'Michael Robartes and the Dancer,' 'Sailing to Byzantium,' and 'Lapis Lazuli' draw on artifacts for their inspiration and theme. It is therefore easy to understand why when Yeats confronts the dilemma of man in his old age faced by the choice between the abstractions of Plato and Plotinus on the one hand, and the intimations of a sensuous reality symbolized by art on the other, he decides in favor of the latter making his "peace / With learned Italian things / And the proud stones of Greece."[14] The voice that speaks to the poet and sculptor of Ireland from under Ben Bulben is the voice of the soul of Yeats from eternity, its former conjectural wisdom now apparently confirmed by the experience of death. It is natural that it should exhort them to follow the tradition of Greek and Renaissance art:

> Poet and sculptor, do the work,
> Nor let the modish painter shirk
> What his great forefathers did.[15]

The poet, painter, sculptor and craftsman, have all the same vision and the same goals. "Pen, chisel or brush" are means to the same ends.

Whenever Yeats thinks of craftsmanship in the arts the figures that come to his imagination are those of the Greek or Roman sculptor, the ancient Byzantine worker in metal or mosaic, the medieval Japanese painter or the Oriental craftsman with his heritage of traditionally developed skill. It is worthwhile inquiring why he finds these types fascinating. Such an enquiry would tell us a great deal about what Yeats considers the essentials of the work of art or the nature of craftsmanship. Typical of this nostalgia for ancient craftsmanship is his desire to have a glimpse of Byzantium:

> I think if I could be given a month of Antiquity and leave to spend it where I chose, I would spend it in Byzantium a little before Justinian opened St. Sophia and closed the Academy of Plato. I think I could find in some little wine-shop some philosophical worker in mosaic who could answer all my questions, the supernatural descending nearer to him than to Plotinus even, for the pride of his delicate skill would make what was an instrument of power to princes and clerics, a murderous madness in the mob, show as a lovely flexible presence like that of a perfect human body.[16]

In contrasting the Byzantine worker with the abstract Plotinus[17] Yeats emphasizes his concreteness. This worker in mosaic for Yeats is "philosophical" in the sense that he combines skill with supernatural vision. It is the combination of these—an exquisite skill with this sensuous vision—that endows his work with the Yeatsian ideal of beauty like that of a "perfectly proportioned human body."[18] It is also an art where the craftsman attains a true impersonality—the anonymity of ancient art suggestive of the total renunciation of his egotistic nature; it expresses that "Unity of Being" which is one of Yeats's favorite ideals in art:

I think that in early Byzantium, never before or since in recorded history, religious, aesthetic and practical life were one, that architect and artificers—though not, it may be, poets, for language had been the instrument of controversy and must have grown abstract—spoke to the multitude and the few alike. The painter, the mosaic worker, the worker in gold and silver, the illuminator of sacred books, were almost impersonal, almost perhaps without the consciousness of individual design, absorbed in their subject-matter and that the vision of the whole people. They could copy out of old Gospel books those pictures that seemed as sacred as the text, and yet weave all into a vast design, the work of many that seemed the work of one, that made building, picture, pattern, metal-work of rail and lamp, seem but a single image.[19]

It is this yearning for a lost horizon both of art and spiritual vision that is the inspiration of the famous poem 'Sailing to Byzantium.' Images of the "gold mosaic of a wall," the "sages" who could be the "singing masters" of his soul, and the "artifice of eternity" suggest his view of the ideal art of the Byzantine craftsman. In its emphasis upon the impersonality of the artist's vision and his spiritual liberation from nature into eternity, Yeats recalls the Byzantine view of supernatural reality:

Once out of nature I shall never take
My bodily form from any natural thing,
But such a form as Grecian goldsmiths make
Of hammered gold and gold enamelling
To keep a drowsy Emperor awake;
Or set upon a golden bough to sing
To lords and ladies of Byzantium
Of what is past, or passing, or to come.[20]

It is this product of Byzantine art that Yeats again recalls as symbols of the superhuman in 'Byzantium':

Miracle, bird or golden handiwork,
More miracle than bird or handiwork,
Planted on the star-lit golden bough,
Can like the cocks of Hades crow,
Or, by the moon embittered, scorn aloud
In glory of changeless metal
Common bird or petal
And all complexities of mire or blood.[21]

If the Byzantine craftsman embodies the ideals that appeal to Yeats in the creative process, its end product and its vision, he frequently turns to the Oriental craftsman for similar values. He finds in the East also the crafts that transcend mere egotistical personality, and enter into the larger heritage of a tradition that is sophisticated in technical mastery and rich in spiritual vision. His desire is to become like the Oriental craftsman in his unselfconscious and spiritual joy in the creative process:

> . . . I wanted to create once more an art where the artist's handiwork would hide as under those half-anonymous chisels or as we find it in some old Scots ballads, or in some twelfth-or thirteenth-century Arthurian Romance. . . . Elaborate modern psychology sounds egotistical, I thought, when it speaks in the first person, but not those simple emotions which resemble the more, the more powerful they are, everybody's emotion, and I was soon to write many poems where an always personal emotion was woven into a general pattern of myth and symbol.[22]

The Fenian poet who says that his heart has grown cold and callous "for thy hapless Fate, dear Ireland, and sorrows of my own" follows tradition, ". . . and if he does not move us deeply it is because he has no sensuous musical vocabulary that comes at need, without compelling him to sedentary toil and so driving him out from his fellows."[23] Yeats's ambition is to create this sensuous vocabulary, and be a link in the chain between the past and the future poets.

It is for this reason that Yeats wants to emulate the medieval Japanese painter:

> I thought to create that sensuous, musical vocabulary, and not for myself only, but that I might leave it to later Irish poets, much as a medieval Japanese painter left his style as an inheritance to his family, and I was careful to use a traditional manner and matter, yet changed by that toil, impelled by my share in Cain's curse, by all that sterile modern complication, by my "originality," as the newspapers call it, did something altogether different.[24]

Sato's gift a "changeless sword" lying on his table brings recollections of Oriental traditional art and its values of hereditary skill and vision. It is symbolic of a world of loveliness or absolute perfection of beauty:

In Sato's house,
Curved like new moon, moon-luminous,
It lay five hundred years.
Yet if no change appears
No moon; only an aching heart
Conceives a changeless work of art.

This symbolic art representing the world of unchanging eternity like the miracle of golden handiwork of Byzantium scorning time is the product of a continuous anonymous or impersonal tradition of Japanese art passed on from father to son:

Our learned men have urged
That when and where 'twas forged
A marvellous accomplishment,
In painting or in pottery, went
From father unto son
And through the centuries ran
And seemed unchanging like the sword.[25]

Yeats is probably thinking of the praise of such art by Ruskin or William Morris. In *The Art of the People* William Morris condemns Western commerce for bringing about the ruin of the traditional and historical arts of the East:

. . . While we are met here in Birmingham, to further the spread of education in art, Englishmen in India are, in their short-sightedness, actively destroying the very sources of that education—jewelry, metal-work, pottery, calico-printing, brocade-weaving, carpet-making—all the famous and historical arts of the great peninsula have been for long treated as matters of no importance, to be thrust aside for the advantage of any paltry scrap of so-called commerce; and matters are now speedily coming to an end there. . . . The often-praised perfection of these arts is the blossom of many ages of labour. . . ."[26]

This art rooted in tradition and anonymous skill is based on a vision of the soul like the art of the philosophical Byzantine metal worker:

Soul's beauty being most adored,
Men and their business took
The soul's unchanging look;
For the most rich inheritor,

> Knowing that none could pass Heaven's door
> That loved inferior art,
> Had such an aching heart
> That he, although a country's talk
> For silken clothes and stately walk,
> Had waking wits; it seemed
> Juno's peacock screamed.[27]

It is the same feeling of cultural continuity in song and metaphor that he feels in Rabindranath Tagore's *Gitanjali*:

> I said, 'In the East you know how to keep a family illustrious. The other day the curator of a Museum pointed to me a little dark-skinned man who was arranging their Chinese prints and said, "That is the hereditary connoisseur of the Mikado, he is the fourteenth of his family to hold the post."[28]

Tagore's poetry rooted in an ancient mystical tradition and popular Indian folklore appears "as much the growth of the common soil as the grass and the rushes." This thought of an art rooted in folklore drawing its strength from the soil "Anteus-like" recurs in Yeats's poem 'The Municipal Gallery Revisited.' Yeats's reading of Tagore reflects his own preoccupation with the nature of traditional and impersonal art:

> A tradition, where poetry and religion are the same thing, has passed through the centuries, gathering from learned and unlearned metaphor and emotion, and carried back again to the multitude the thought of the scholar and of the noble.[29]

Tagore has been content to "discover the soul and surrender himself to its spontaneity."[30] He finds an innocence and simplicity in him:

> At times I wonder if he has it from the literature of Bengal or from religion, and at other times, remembering the birds alighting on his brother's hands, I find pleasure in thinking it hereditary, a mystery that was growing through the centuries like the courtesy of a Tristan or a Pelanore.[31]

What is common to the Byzantine mosaic worker, the medieval Japanese painter and the Oriental craftsman in Yeats's view is the inspiration they derive from a vision of the supernatural and traditional craftsmanship. These artists become the medium or the hierophants of this religious or mystical experience. A certain demonic myth comes to Yeats as he views their work, and its intensity. All art objects have for him intimations of a reality beyond the world of time and Nature. He says in *Rosa Alchemica* that he had gathered round him objects of art—Crivelli, antique bronze gods and goddesses, books bound in leather, stamped with intricate design and of a carefully chosen color:

> All those forms: that Madonna with her brooding purity, those delighted ghostly faces under the morning light, those bronze divinities with their passionless dignity, those wild shapes rushing from despair to despair, belonged to a divine world wherein I had no part; and every experience, however profound, every perception, however exquisite, would bring me the bitter dream of a limitless energy I could never know, and even in my most perfect moment I would be two selves, the one watching with heavy eyes the other's moment of content.[32]

Following Ruskin and William Morris, Yeats does not make any distinction between the poet and the craftsman. As Ruskin says, no arbitrary line can be drawn "between making statues and making toys, between designing cathedrals and designing plows." All great art is a fusion of vision and craftsmanship: "a blacksmith may put soul into the making of a horse-shoe and an architect may put none in the building of a church. Only exactly in proportion the soul is thrown into it, the art becomes Fine. . . . Art is the operation of the hand and the intelligence together."[33] It is this "operation of the hand and the intelligence" that constitutes the essence of art for Yeats. Yeats has numerous statements on this subject expressing his conviction that all art begins and ends in spiritual revelation. The life of the artist for him is in the old Biblical saying, "'The wind bloweth where it listeth, and thou hearest the sound thereof, but canst not tell whence it cometh and whither it goeth; so is every one that is born of the Spirit.'"[34] He expresses the same sense of mystery of art elsewhere, ". . . romance, poetry, intellectual beauty, is the only signal that the supreme Enchanter, or some one in His councils, is speaking of what has been, and shall be again, in the consummation of time."[35] Yeats's conviction in this matter closely follows Blake. The former speaks of the "Divine Arts of Imagination," and writing on his idea of inspiration, Yeats says:

> William Blake expounds the history of inspiration by a very curious and obscure symbol. A lark, he says, mounts upward into the heart of the heavens, and there is met by another and descending lark, which touches its wings to its wings; and he would have us understand, . . . that man attains spiritual influence in like fashion. He must go on perfecting earthly power and perception until they are so subtilised that divine power and divine perception descend to meet them, and the song of earth and the song of heaven mingle together.[36]

While Yeats reaffirms in his own way the traditional Platonic idea of inspiration as divine frenzy,[37] still what distinguishes his poetic theory and practice is his equally firm demand that the craft of poetry involves the same intense labor and dedication of the craftsman working on metal or mosaic. It is this insistence on the union of inspiration with conscious and persistent labor or toil that Yeats combines a traditional view of poetry with a more modern one insisted on by poets and critics like Ezra Pound and T.S. Eliot.[38] Indeed Yeats states clearly that the old theory of inspiration by itself is inadequate:

> How often do I not hear in this country that literature is to be achieved by some kind of mysterious visitation of God, which makes it needless for us to labour at the literary art, and hearing this long for one hour among my books with the great Flaubert, who talked of art, art and again art, or with Blake, who held that life itself became an art when wisely lived. When I hear this kind of talk I am inclined to say that being inspired by God is a profession that is full, so many men have I met who have held themselves to be thus visited. Alas the inspiration of God, which is, indeed, the source of all which is greatest in the world, comes only to him who labours at rhythm and cadence, at form and style, until they have no secret hidden from him. This art we must learn from the old literatures of the world. . . . We have shrunk from the labour that art demands, and have made thereby our best moments of no account. We must learn from the literatures of France and England to be supreme artists and then God will send to us supreme inspiration.[39]

The words "labour," "toil," and "sedentary toil," acquire special connotation in Yeats's idiom both in his prose and verse. The creative process is an imitation of the creator of the universe. The labor of God is a concept expressive of this sanctity in arduous work dedicated to the creation of beautiful forms. Again following Blake in his statement that "the flower is the labour of ages," Yeats says that while God yawns in earthquake and thunder and popular displays, "he toils in rounding the delicate spiral of a shell."[40] The thought and image recur in the lines:

> To round that shell's elaborate whorl,
> Adorning every secret track
> With the delicate mother-of-pearl,
> Made the joints of Heaven crack.[41]

The symbol of God's labor haunts Yeats's mind: ". . . and the face of Princess Margaretha full of subtle beauty, emotional and precise, and impassive with a still intensity suggesting that final consummate strength which rounds the spiral of a shell."[42] Thus God in his infinite labor, the strenuous efforts of the sculptor or the metal worker in Byzantium or the Orient and the poet are all akin in their strenuous effort to create beauty. This is a view that recalls Carlyle's well known statement that genius is the infinite capacity for taking pains. This consecration of labor in the medieval craftsman is the theme of William Morris who said "I have only one subject to lecture on—the relation of Art to Labour." Speaking of this kind of labor which rejoices in the creation of beauty, Morris added, ". . . no man will any longer have an excuse for talking about the curse of labour, no man will any longer have an excuse for evading the blessing of labour."[43] When Yeats speaks of "Adam's Curse" he uses the word "curse" in an ambiguous sense in which the curse is also a blessing; if it is Adam's curse, it is also the curse under which God suffers in the creation of the shell; in reality it is the dedication of the artist to a life of intense labor for the sake of his work. The sense of the beautiful is a vision; it requires toil to be realized:

> 'To be born woman is to know—
> Although they do not talk of it at school—
> That we must labour to be beautiful.'

If beauty is thus an effect requiring labor, love too is a vision which "needs much labouring":

> There have been lovers who thought love should be
> So much compounded of high courtesy

That they would sigh and quote with learned looks
Precedents out of beautiful old books.

The poet's vision too requires the same exacting labor, though the finished product may have about it an apparent spontaneity concealing the effort:

'A line will take us hours maybe;
Yet if it does not seem a moment's thought,
Our stitching and unstitching has been naught.
Better go down upon your marrow-bones
And scrub a kitchen pavement, or break stones
Like an old pauper, in all kinds of weather;
For to articulate sweet sounds together
Is to work harder than all these, and yet
Be thought an idler by the noisy set
Of bankers, schoolmasters, and clergymen
The martyrs call the world.'

The art of the dancer—in many ways symbolic for Yeats—is the art that conceals art. It is in dance that Yeats finds the perfect coalescence of vision and craft, the highest moment of existence called the fifteenth phase in his *Vision* "where all thought becomes an image."[44] It is in dance that Adam's curse becomes a blossom like the flower created by God's labor; the effort and the achievement are unified as body and soul become one, while at the same time toil and art are in indivisible harmony:

Labour is blossoming or dancing where
The body is not bruised to pleasure soul,
Nor beauty born out of its own despair,
Nor blear-eyed wisdom out of midnight oil.
O Chestnut-tree, great-rooted blossomer,
Are you the leaf, the blossom or the bole?
O body swayed to music, O brightening glance,
How can we know the dancer from the dance?[45]

This creative labor as applied to the art of poetry has for its aim the making of a poem correspond as closely as possible to the work of a medieval or Oriental craftsman, for to Yeats as we have noticed already, the archetype of all art alike in inspiration and precision is the handiwork. It is in this sense he speaks of the "craft of verse"[46]—a phrase that has to be understood in the context of his interpretation of or response to the world of handicrafts combining a visionary element and a most severe discipline or exacting labor. Yeats praises Robert Gregory for possessing this virtue:

> We dreamed that a great painter had been born
> To cold Clare rock and Galway rock and thorn,
> To that stern colour and that delicate line
> That are our secret discipline
> Where the gazing heart doubles her might.[47]

In thus making a poem approximate to an object of art of another kind, Yeats emphasizes certain fundamental requirements.

The basic necessity for an artist in his view is the stock of traditional wisdom, experience and speculation embodied in the folklore or mythology of a race or a culture. It is to this that the poet like the craftsman must turn for his subject-matter and its emotional or imaginative significance. Like Matthew Arnold, who insists on the relevance of the Greek myths to the modern poet and his audience,[48] Yeats repeatedly emphasizes the need for the poet to draw upon this vast storehouse of accumulated story, myth and thought, in what he calls the "book of the people." This book of the people is the poet's scripture:

> Folk-lore is at once the Bible, the Thirty-nine Articles, and the Book of Common Prayer, and well-nigh all the great poets have lived by its light. Homer, Aeschylus, Sophocles, Shakespeare, and even Dante, Goethe, and Keats, were little more than folk-lorists with musical tongues.[49]

A poet must again labor to identify himself with this traditional voice in a sort of exhausting effort to get rid of his modern psychological ego: a mythology invented by a poet cannot have the broad base of an inherited folk-lore with which he identifies himself:

> No conscious invention can take the place of tradition, for he who would write a folk tale, and thereby bring a new life into literature, must have the fatigue of the spade in his hands and the stupor of the fields in his heart. Let us listen humbly to the old people telling their stories, and perhaps God will send the primitive excellent imagination into the midst of us again.[50]

Elsewhere he writes; "Of all the many things the past bequeaths to the future, the greatest are great legends; they are the mothers of nations."[51] In these legends all the joys and sorrows of life and the primary human affections find their appropriate or adequate expression:

> There is no passion, no vague desire, no tender longing that cannot find fit type or symbol in the legends of the peasantry or in the traditions of the scalds and the gleeman.
> . . .
> All these stories are such as to unite man more closely to the woods and hills and waters about him, and to the birds and animals that live in them, and to give him types and symbols for those feelings and passions which find no adequate expression in common life.[52]

In addition to the primary human affections the longings of man's soul are also precisely expressed in these legends:

> Emotions which seem vague or extravagant when expressed under the influence of modern literature, cease to be vague and extravagant when associated with ancient legend and mythology, for legend and mythology were born out of man's longing for the mysterious and the infinite.[53]

It is thus that folklore and myth become for Yeats a kind of Bible for the imagination of the poet who can thus find the religion he needs in an age in which orthodox beliefs are under attack by science:

> . . . deprived by Huxley and Tyndall, whom I detested, of the simple-minded religion of my childhood, I had made a new religion, almost an infallible church of poetic tradition, of a fardel of stories, and of personages, and of emotions, inseparable from their first expression, passed on from generation to generation by poets and painters with some help from philosophers and theologians.[54]

In seeking to make poetry thus a religious experience drawing upon the accumulated folklore and myths of the ages, Yeats emphasizes the use of the symbol as the central means of evocative spiritual communication. Alongside with or as an essential part of folklore is a world of traditional symbols coming from the primitive imagination of mankind. These symbols contain esoteric meanings reaching out to the infinite in man and Nature:

It is only by ancient symbols, by symbols that have numberless meanings besides the one or two the writer lays an emphasis upon, or the half-score he knows of, that any highly subjective art can escape from the barrenness and shallowness of a too conscious arrangement, into the abundance and depth of Nature. The poet of essences and pure ideas must seek in the half-lights that glimmer from symbol to symbol as if to the ends of the earth, all that the epic and the dramatic poet finds of mystery and shadow in the accidental circumstances of life.[55]

Elsewhere he says that the symbol is the "only possible expression of some invisible essence, a transparent lamp about a spiritual essence, a transparent lamp about a spiritual flame."[56] In these symbols there is the "Memory of Nature" or "The Great Memory," and it is through them that the imagination communicates with the world of the spirit. Magic, poetry and the arts have therefore used symbols for the purpose of conjuring up vision:

I cannot now think symbols less than the greatest of all powers whether they are used consciously by the masters of magic, or half unconsciously by their successors, the poet, the musician and the artist. . . . Whatever the passions of man have gathered about, becomes a symbol in the Great Memory, and in the hands of him who has the secret it is a worker of wonders, a caller-up of angels or of devils.[57]

While Yeats's ideas of symbolism are drawn from various sources—Plato, Plotinus, the Kabbalah, and the Smaragdine tablet, *The Upanishads* and Buddhism—still his writings show a deep familiarity as we have already seen with the use of symbolism by the Byzantine metal worker, the goldsmith, the sculptor, and in particular by the Oriental artisan. The use of the symbol in the imaginative arts results in a certain aesthetic distance disposing the mind of the onlooker towards a contemplative attitude:

. . . the arts which interest me, while seeming to separate from the world and us a group of figures, images, symbols, enable us to pass for a few moments into a deep of the mind that had hitherto been too subtle for our habitation. As a deep of the mind can only be approached through what is most human, most delicate, we should distrust bodily distance, mechanism, and loud noise.[58]

It is this aesthetic or imaginative distance that Yeats finds in Asiatic craftsmanship and its use of the language of the symbol. "It may be well," he says, "if we go to school in Asia for the distance from life in European art has come from little but difficulty with material."[59] He must go to Asia for the kind of art he wants to create in poetry and drama; he turns to the mask and symbolism of the Japanese Noh Play. He finds greater appeal in the dead figures of the East than in the "vitality" of realistic art: "It is even possible that being is only possessed completely by the dead, and that it is some knowledge of this that makes us gaze with so much emotion upon the face of the Sphinx or of a Buddha."[60] In language that recalls Thoreau's *Walden*, Yeats urges European artists to turn to the East, "Europe is very old and has seen many arts run through the circle and has learned the fruit of every flower and known what this fruit sends up, and it is now time to copy the East and live deliberately."[61]

A close analysis of this fascination of Yeats for the world of the craftsman reveals that his ideals in poetry are shaped by his intense life-long study and appreciation of their work. While he speaks frequently of Western traditions in the arts and crafts, he also makes significant references to traditional Oriental skills in the same field. The Oriental craftsman becomes for Yeats an ideal or an archetypal figure of the artist. Yeats was especially fascinated by the anonymity of Oriental art with its roots in spiritual vision and the development of its skill based on a hereditary tradition. It is these characteristics that he aspires to embody in his poems. Several critics[62] have emphasized the sources of his philosophy in Buddhism and Theosophy.[63] While it is true that these had a shaping influence on his philosophy, it is his knowledge of and admiration for the arts and crafts of the Orient that in part shape his ideals as a poet at work on the making of a poem. This influence has yet to receive adequate attention from critics. An analysis of his comments on Eastern art will help us to understand some important aspects of his theory and practice as a poet. Further it will help us to connect it with the Oriental element in his philosophy. To a spiritualist like Yeats it is only natural that the philosophies and religions of the East should have a profound appeal. A good example of this is his poem entitled 'Lapis Lazuli.' In its highly stylized carving, in its attitude of the infinite soul gazing on mundane scenes of change and flux, and its suggestion of tragic joy represented in terms of a small carved stone, Yeats finds an archetype of all symbolic art:

> Two Chinamen, behind them a third,
> Are carved in lapis lazuli,
> Over them flies a long-legged bird,
> A symbol of longevity;
> The third, doubtless a serving-man,
> Carries a musical instrument.
>
> Every discoloration of the stone,
> Every accidental crack or dent,
> Seems a water-course or an avalanche,
> Or lofty slope where it still snows
> Though doubtless plum or cherry-branch
> Sweetens the little half-way house
> Those Chinamen climb towards, and I
> Delight to imagine them seated there;
> There, on the mountain and the sky,
> On all the tragic scene they stare.
> One asks for mournful melodies;
> Accomplished fingers begin to play.
> Their eyes mid many wrinkles, their eyes,
> Their ancient, glittering eyes, are gay.

Though drawn to the East by its philosophy and art, still Yeats however could not accept its abstract nihilistic tendencies of thought or speculation.[64] He protests against the "Buddha's emptiness"—probably alluding to the ideal of emptying the mind of all images recommended by the Buddha—and against "All Asiatic vague immensities." From these he wants to turn to the reality of "minute particulars" and to a world of rich sensuous and concrete imagery. Even his supernatural world is sensuous; it is only the natural world raised to a higher perfection of being in eternity, and not its total contradiction. The *Vision* is essentially a sensuous myth based on the cyclic phases of the moon. The soul and the body are not antithetical. Like Blake, Yeats takes the body to be that part of the soul which we see with our naked eye. Thus in the fifteenth phase of the Moon, an ideal perfection is attained in which body and soul are at once in their fullness of beauty—a fullness of beauty beyond the empirical world of imperfect manifestation:

> All thought becomes an image and the soul
> Becomes a body: that body and that soul

Too perfect at the full to lie in a cradle,
Too lonely for the traffic of the world:
Body and soul cast out and cast away
Beyond the visible world.[65]

Thus for the poet "all dreams of the soul / End in a beautiful man's or woman's body." The theme of 'The Tower' is the debate between abstract philosophy and concrete or sensuous mysticism of the poet's imagination. Yeats begins by wondering whether because of his age he should now abandon the sensuous world of "excited, passionate, fantastical Imagination" of "ear and eye":

It seems that I must bid the Muse go pack,
Choose Plato and Plotinus for a friend
Until imagination, ear and eye,
Can be content with argument and deal
In abstract things; or be derided by
A sort of battered kettle at the heel.

The poem ends by a declaration of Yeats's faith in the sensuous world as foreshadowing the superhuman:

I mock Plotinus' thought
And cry in Plato's teeth,
Death and life were not
Till man made up the whole,
Made lock, stock and barrel
Out of his bitter soul,
Aye, sun and moon and star, all,
And further add to that
That, being dead, we rise,
Dream and so create
Translunar Paradise.

It is this semi-mystical sensuous intuition of reality that makes Yeats choose for himself the ideal form wrought by a Grecian goldsmith of hammered gold and gold enamelling or that of a golden bird on a golden bough. He dwells on this idea again in 'Byzantium.'

Miracle, bird or golden handiwork,
More miracle than bird or handiwork,

Planted on the star-lit golden bough,
Can like the cocks of Hades crow,
Or, by the moon embittered, scorn aloud
In glory of changeless metal
Common bird or petal
And all complexities of mire or blood.

Some superhuman craftsman or soul-smith is at work making these souls: the metaphor of the smith at work as in Blake's 'Tyger' is characteristic, "The smithies break the flood, / The golden smithies of the Emperor!" In the sequence of "Those images that yet / Fresh images beget" we have Yeats's idea of a poem approximating to the concrete work of a craftsman or an artist eliminating all abstract statements.

Indeed the touchstone for a well-made poem for him is a material artifact, precisely because the latter can represent the fullness of a concrete existence uncorrupted by abstraction. It is this ideal that makes for pure beauty for him. Michael Robartes recommends it to the dancer, and when the dancer asks him, "And must no beautiful woman be / Learned like a man?" he replies,

Paul Veronese
And all his sacred company
Imagined bodies all their days
By the lagoon you love so much,
For proud, soft, ceremonious proof
That all must come to sight and touch;
While Michael Angelo's Sistine roof,
His 'Morning' and his 'Night' disclose
How sinew that has been pulled tight,
Or it may be loosened in repose,
Can rule by supernatural right
Yet be but sinew.

Michael Robartes quotes the Bible against this dichotomy of the body and the soul:

Did God in portioning wine and bread
Give man His thought or His mere body?
. . .
I have principles to prove me right.

Any abstract thought that cannot be absorbed by a woman's physical beauty must be rejected by her:

> That blest souls are not composite,
> And that all beautiful women may
> Live in uncomposite blessedness,
> And lead us to the like—if they
> Will banish every thought, unless
> The lineaments that please their view
> When the long looking-glass is full,
> Even from the foot-sole think it too.

Yeats's description of Maud Gonne's beauty expresses this idea:

> Her beauty backed by her great stature . . . was incredibly distinguished, . . . her face, like the face of some Greek statue, showed little thought, her whole body seemed a master work of long labouring thought, as though a Scopus had measured and calculated, consorted with Egyptian sages, and mathematicians out of Babylon, that he might outface even Artemisia's sepulchral image with a living norm.[66]

Yeats's poem 'Woman's Beauty is like a frail Bird' also contains the image of bodily perfection wrought by centuries of labor:

> How many centuries spent
> The sedentary soul
> In toils of measurement
> Beyond eagle or mole,
> Beyond hearing or seeing,
> Or Archimides guess
> To raise into being
> That loveliness?
>
> A strange, unserviceable thing,
> A fragile, exquisite, pale shell,
> That the vast troubled waters bring
> To the loud sands before day has broken
> The storm arose and suddenly fell
> Amid the dark before day had broken
> What death? what discipline?

In 'Ego Dominus Tuus' he opposes the "modern hope" by which we emphasize the "gentle, sensitive mind" to the "old nonchalance of hand" which we have lost. The result is an intellectualized or self-conscious or cerebral art; sculpture, poetry and painting are all infected by this disease:

> Whether we have chosen chisel, pen or brush,
> We are but critics, or but half create,
> Timid, entangled, empty and abashed.

In the context the masonic metaphor of Dante as a sculptor "setting his chisel to the hardest stone" comes naturally to Yeats because of his habitual thinking of the poet as a craftsman. Hence it is that the poet is represented as "seeking an image and not a book." This is his poetic intuition of reality as made up of concrete images; he regards abstraction as a fall of the imagination from its vision of sensuous beauty to an intellectual level. Thus a poem based on this vision must be imagistic; it must exclude all abstractions or whatever abstraction cannot be subsumed in its concrete quality. It must have a woman's ideal beauty which is uncomposite in its blessedness; it has the inseparable union of body and thought as the symbolic wine and bread of Christ's body. A woman's beauty can be marred by abstract argument, or opinion:

> Have I not seen the loveliest woman born
> Out of the mouth of Plenty's horn,
> Because of her opinionated mind
> Barter that horn and every good
> By quiet natures understood
> For an old bellows full of angry wind?[67]

If a woman's beauty is thus spoiled by her "opinions" the body of a poem or its beauty can be ruined by its abstractions. It is this habit of Yeats's imagination, or this definition of the beautiful in art, that makes him emphasize the use of the image in the structure of a poem.

Against this background of his thought, we can understand his comparison of a poem to "the perfectly proportioned human body." It explains Yeats's insistence on what Ezra Pound describes as the "sculpture of rhyme." The sense of poetic form, the need for structure in verse, and the adherence to traditional stanzaic patterns and to regular meters are all aspects of his imaginative effort to give a poem its well proportioned body. Yeatsian metaphors for poetry are frequently drawn from the world of sculpture, and the essence of sculpture is measurement. Greek art triumphed because of its sculptors who brought Pythagorean numbers and measure to their creation, and it was this adherence to measure that gave the work of Phidias its supreme sensuous beauty:

> No! Greater than Pythagoras, for the men
> That with a mallet or a chisel modelled these
> Calculations that look but casual flesh, put down
> All Asiatic vague immensities,
> And not the banks of oars that swam upon
> The many-headed foam at Salamis.
> Europe put off that foam when Phidias
> Gave women dreams and dreams their looking-glass.[68]

Yeats alludes to the influence of Greek sculpture on the Gandhara school of Indian art, and the tendency of this school to make sculpture of the Buddha an Oriental Apollo:[69]

> One image crossed the many-headed, sat
> Under the tropic shade, grew round and slow,
> No Hamlet thin from eating flies, a fat
> Dreamer of the Middle Ages. Empty eyeballs knew
> That knowledge increases unreality, that
> Mirror on mirror mirrored is all the show.
> When gong and conch declare the hour to bless
> Grimalkin crawls to Buddha's emptiness.[70]

The art of Ireland must be a synthesis of the sensuousness of Greek sculpture and the spirituality of Indian art. Yeats's plea for such a synthesis, and his condemnation of formless art without measurement are addressed as his last admonition to Irish artists:

> We Irish, born into that ancient sect
> But thrown upon this filthy modern tide
> And by its formless spawning fury wrecked,
> Climb to our proper dark, that we may trace
> The lineaments of a plummet-measured face.[71]

The need for conforming to measurement is emphasized in his testament addressed to "poet and sculptor" (the phrase is significant in the context of Yeats's idea of form in poetry and sculpture as analogous);

Poet and sculptor, do the work,
Nor let the modish painter shirk
What his great forefathers did,
Bring the soul of man to God.
Make him fill the cradles right.

Measurement began our might:
Forms a stark Egyptian thought,
Forms that gentler Phidias wrought.[72]

Yeats traces the history of European art from the Renaissance to the present as a decline from a sense of disciplined form to formlessness. From Michelangelo through the Quattrocento to Calvert, Wilson, Blake and Claude, this "greater dream" prevailed "but after that / Confusion fell upon our thought." His exhortation to poets is to return to the tradition of the well-made poem, and recover the old measurements; poets must again learn their "trade":

Irish poets, learn your trade,
Sing whatever is well made,
Scorn the sort now growing up
All out of shape from toe to top,
Their unremembering hearts and heads
Base-born products of base beds.[73]

This explains why Yeats regards free verse with contempt. Condemning Henley's free verse he says, "I disagreed with him about everything,. . . . With the exception of some early poems founded upon old French models I disliked his poetry, mainly because he wrote in vers-libre, which I associated with Tyndal and Huxley, and Bastien-Lepage's clownish peasant staring with vacant eyes at her great boots."[74] On the contrary Yeats needed some traditional form, some old inherited metrical pattern: "I wanted the strongest passions, passions that had nothing to do with observation, and metrical forms that seemed old enough to have been sung by men half-asleep or riding upon a journey."[75] He says he seeks a "powerful and passionate syntax"

and a complete coincidence between period and stanza. Because I need a passionate syntax for passionate subject-matter I compel myself to accept those traditional metres that have developed with the language. Ezra

Pound, Turner, Lawrence wrote admirable free verse, I could not, I would lose myself, become joyless like those mad old women.[76]

If on the one hand he finds in traditional metrical pattern a rule that corresponds to number and measurement in sculpture he finds in an inherited meter a kind of mask for the voice—a mask which enables him to rid himself of his own egotistical self, and attain the pure impersonality of the craftsman or the sculptor:

If I wrote of personal love or sorrow in free verse, or in any rhythm that left it unchanged, amid all its accidence, I would be full of self-contempt because of my egotism and indiscretion, and foresee the boredom of my reader. I must choose a traditional stanza, even what I alter must seem traditional. I commit my emotion to shepherds, herdsmen, cameldrivers, learned men, Milton's or Shelley's Platonist, that tower Palmer drew. Talk to me of originality and I will turn on you with rage. I am a crowd, I am a lonely man, I am nothing.[77]

According to Yeats all that is personal soon rots; it must be packed in ice or salt. "Ancient salt is best packing." Traditional meter is this salt. Passion gives a form of art its living quality; its form gives it its timeless permanence. A work of art is thus a paradox of passion which is mutable and of art which is permanent or is a compound of opposites. It is this combination that makes it at once "cold and passionate." This paradoxical phrase is also a variation of Yeats's familiar theme of the need to combine excitement with the discipline of labor; the comparison of a poem to a cold and passionate dawn recalls his idea of the creator as an artisan who combines inspiration and labor:

The maid of honour whose tragedy they sing must be lifted out of history with timeless pattern, she is one of the four Maries, the rhythm is old and familiar, imagination must dance, must be carried beyond feeling into the aboriginal ice. Is ice the correct word? I once boasted, copying the phrase from a letter of my father's, that I would write a poem 'cold and passionate as the dawn.'[78]

It is meter which in poetry corresponds to measurement in sculpture. It acts like a mask for the speaker's voice. It helps the fusion of calculation and number with intense feeling so creating the ideal poem or work of art which is at once "cold and passionate as the dawn." Moreover traditional verse is a fusion of the past and the present, and therefore stands for a timeless experience. Like myth, symbol or image, a traditional verse pattern is also a means of recapturing some great memory. It has a symbolic function in a poem:

> When I speak blank verse and analyze my feelings, I stand at a moment of history when instinct, its traditional songs and dances, its general agreement, is of the past. I have been cast up out of the whale's belly though I still remember the sound and sway that came from beyond its ribs, and, like the Queen in Paul Fort's ballad, I smell of the fish of the sea. The contrapuntal structure of the verse, to employ a term adopted by Robert Bridges, combines the past and the present.[79]

If poetry is akin to sculpture in its bodily measurement, and meter is part of this body of a pocm, rhythm too for Ycats is an csscntially sensuous perception. When he speaks of it he associates it with the idea of a concrete body: "Rhythm implies a living body, a breast to rise and fall, or limbs that dance."[80] Indeed he finds an opposition between the rhythmic and the abstract. Once again the touchstone of Oriental art comes to his mind; "I think Keats perhaps greater than Shelley and beyond words greater than Swinburne because he makes pictures one cannot forget and sees them as full of rhythm as a Chinese painting."[81] Explaining the idea he says:

> I separate the rhythmical and the abstract. They are brothers but one is Abel and one is Cain. In poetry they are confused for we know that poetry is rhythm, but in music hall verses we find an abstract cadence, which is vulgar because it is apart from imitation. This cadence is a mechanism, it never suggests a voice shaken with joy or sorrow as poetical rhythm does. It is but the noise of a machine and not the coming and going of the breath.[82]

As art is a vision of reality that can lead us to a contemplative state of mind, rhythm must be subservient to this purpose. Poetry must be purified by casting out descriptions of nature for the sake of description, the brooding of scientific opinion as in Tennyson or the moral law for the sake of moral law. Poetry must return to the use of symbolism for inducing states of reverie or meditation:

With this change of substance, this return to imagination, this understanding that the laws of art, which are the hidden laws of the world, can alone bind the imagination, would come a change of style, and we would cast out of serious poetry those energetic rhythms, as of a man running, which are the invention of the will with its eyes always on something to be done or undone; and we would seek out those wavering, meditative, organic rhythms, which are the embodiment of the imagination, that neither desires nor hates, because it has done with time, and only wishes to gaze upon some reality, some beauty; nor would it be any longer possible for anybody to deny the importance of form, in all its kinds.[83]

This "embodiment of the imagination" requires a rhythm and language different from what we use for expounding an opinon or for describing a thing, ". . . you cannot give a body" Yeats says, "to something that moves beyond the sense, unless your words are as subtle, as complex as full of mysterious life, as the body of a flower or of a woman."[84] The function of rhythm is to sustain the trance-like state induced by the poem:

The purpose of rhythm, it has always seemed to me, is to prolong the moment of contemplation, the moment when we are both asleep and awake, which is the one moment of creation, by hushing us with an alluring monotony, while it holds us waking by variety, to keep us in that state of perhaps real trance, in which the mind liberated from the pressure of the will is unfolded in symbols.[85]

If meter and rhythm are essential components of the structure of a poem, a poet's vocabulary also helps in the spell the poem casts on the reader. Words have a tradition behind them, and a poet must be alive to this heritage of vocabulary:

A poetical passage cannot be understood without a rich memory, and like the older school of painting appeals to a tradition, and that not merely when it speaks of 'Lethe wharf' or 'Dido on the wild sea banks' but in rhythm, in vocabulary; for the ear must notice slight variations upon old cadences and customary words, all that high breeding of poetical style where there is nothing ostentatious, nothing crude, no breath of parvenu or journalist.[86]

The pursuit of style in literature came to be associated in the minds of late nineteenth century writers and critics with a semi-religious or mystical experience.[87] Style becomes an intense spiritual experience, and a meticulous ritual of sound and word in poetry, based on an occult awareness of the magical qualities of expression. Though Yeats's style changed from his early work to the later poems, still his sense of the traditional sanctity and loveliness of words remains with him to the end. Walter Pater is in a sense the high priest of this exaltation of the principle of soul operating in style. As Yeats says:

> . . . we looked consciously to Pater for our philosophy. . . . Pater had said, "Everything that has occupied man, for any length of time, is worthy of our study." Perhaps it was because of Pater's influence that we with affectation of learning, claimed the whole past of literature for our authority, . . . that we were traditional alike in our dress, in our manner, in our opinions, and in our style.[88]

Michael Robartes makes fun of Yeats for writing in "that extravagant style he had learnt from Pater." In spite of these changes, Yeats's feeling for the magic of words is an abiding element in all his work. Yeats is familiar with traditional Oriental methods of inducing trance-like states through incantation or repetition of mystic sounds.[89] "Words alone are certain good" he writes in the 'Song of the Happy Shepherd,' and recalls the mystical *Logos* or *Aum* that was in the beginning:

> The wandering earth herself may be
> Only a sudden flaming word,
> In clanging space a moment heard,
> Troubling the endless reverie.

In the cultivation of style Yeats thus unites a spiritual or magical attitude towards the power of words with a sense of their traditional beauty. He speaks of the need to emphasize the latter; as in the Orient a writer must master the craft of words derived from tradition:

> In life courtesy and self-possession, and in the arts style, are the sensible impressions of the free mind, for both arise out of a deliberate shaping of all things, and from never being swept away, whatever the emotion, into confusion or dullness. The Japanese have numbered with heroic things courtesy at all times whatsoever, and though a writer, who has to withdraw so much of his thought out of his life that he may learn his craft, may find many his betters in daily courtesy, he should never be without style, which is but high breeding in words and in argument."[90]

Yeats's ideas of poetic style changed from his early incantatory manner to his later dramatic quality. He remarks on the change:

> I made my song a coat
> Covered with embroideries
> Out of old mythologies
> From heel to throat;
> But the fools caught it,
> Wore it in the world's eyes
> As though they'd wrought it,
> Song, let them take it,
> For there's more enterprise
> In walking naked.[91]

However beneath this change there is a certain continuity in the sense that he often fuses together the two idioms of traditional and contemporary speech as for example in 'Among School Children,' 'Byzantium,' 'The Statues' and 'Under Ben Bulben.' The emphasis on the use of sensuous or concrete words in poetry increases, while the fusion of contemporary idiom with traditional metrical patterns and rhythmic periods in syntax restrains his style from becoming completely contemporary. It is thus that "passion and precision" are combined in his finest poems.

We can now see why Yeats makes the typical medieval or Oriental craftsman more or less his mask as a poet. The work of the craftsman becomes for him the touchstone of a poem in many important respects. In particular they have in common a vision of the supernatural on the one hand and an intense and exacting or deliberate labor on the other. Thus Yeats combines the old Platonic idea of divine inspiration as the source of art with modern emphasis on the conscious and deliberate creative process. Indeed the inspiration and the labor are seen by him as parts of a single whole. Other poets too have often labored to perfect their style or form. But in Yeats the labor takes on a priest-like quality as the "little ritual of his verse resembles the great ritual of Nature, and becomes mysterious and inscrutable. He becomes . . . a vessel of the creative power of god."[92] It is this sanctity of labor in the medieval craftsman that fascinates him. That is why his repeated emphasis on toil is significant. His drafts as explained by Parkinson[93] and Stallworthy[94] show him often beginning with a prose draft of his ideas, and then transforming it into verse. Very often between the first draft and the final execution there is the same relation that we find in the art of engraving or painting where the first sketch is the starting point for the execution of the final product. These prose drafts are similar to the drawing in pencil that a painter makes before he starts laying on the coloring.

One significant trend in the development of Yeats's symbolism is the movement from the use of symbols drawn from the world of nature in his early poetry to the use of symbols drawn from the world of the arts and crafts in his later poetry. The early poems have a profusion of symbols such as tree, bird, island, leaves, wind, rose, lily, whereas the later poems draw upon statuary, in poems like 'The Statues,' 'A Bronze Head,' 'The Municipal Gallery Revisited' and upon carvings in 'Lapis Lazuli.' This development accompanied Yeats's increasing interest in the world of the arts. In the symbols of nature there is not the same inseparable and permanent unity of thought and image. The symbolic meaning of a tree or a flower is a projection from the mind of man, and it is always somewhat variable and arbitrary. While for Yeats, the rose may mean Sensuous Beauty, Battle, Peace, Ireland and a number of associated ideas, the rose is a rose is a rose to another person. On the contrary a symbol like a statue or lapis lazuli has a core of permanent suggestion inherent in and always inseparable from it. Its symbolism is more universal than that of a natural object. Another reason for this change in Yeats's symbols is that Nature is a world of decay and death from which even its most symbolic objects are not exempt. As Yeats moves away from nature identifying it with decay to the world of the supernatural, the art object (though in its turn subject to decay) becomes for him a type of eternity in its relative permanence and repose. This transition from the world of Nature to that of art, the former symbolizing death and the latter immortality, is the theme of the 'Byzantium' poems. Thus broadly speaking we recognize three stages in Yeats's development as a symbolist: the early abundance of symbols from Nature, a second stage in which Nature is rejected for eternity and the representation of eternity in art, and the last phase where the world of the arts totally replaces Nature. For Yeats the symbol of the dancer is the type of reality in the fifteenth phase of the moon where absolute perfection is attained in the fusion of thought and image. In some of his later poems he therefore uses the image of the dancer.

Even in the case of the dancer the person dancing is after all separable from the dance, though at the moment of the dance itself the two may appear one and the same. But art objects like a statue or lapis lazuli are even more expressive symbols of the ideal phase of reality as the thought and image have become forever one in them.

It is therefore easy to understand why a poem for him should imitate a handiwork, and the poet be like a craftsman. In this process Yeats's style and imagery move away from the early vagueness to their later precision and objectivity. The change in Yeats's style of poetry has several causes like the general change in poetic idiom brought about by the Imagists, his own experience of dramatic work, and the general mood of reaction against Victorian mellifluousness, and the growing anti-romantic attitude of the time. However it can be explained also by this increasing desire in him to make a poem conform to the full concreteness in a work of art like a statue or a carving. We have only to sample phrases in his later work to feel this change. Here are some phrases in his early poems: "phantom Beauty in a mist of tears,"[95] "where windy surges wend,"[96] "when eve has hushed the feathered ways, / With vapoury footsole by the water's drowsy blaze,"[97] "a whirling and a wandering fire,"[98] and "the tall thought-woven sails."[99] Critics of Yeats have commented on his half-Shelleyan twilight idiom of vague meanings, and his addiction to words like "dream," "dim," "pale," "wind," and "cloud" in his early poems. The contrast between this style and his later style accompanies his use of symbols. The later poems of Yeats have what Blake called "a wiry bounding line," a clarity of symbol and meaning, a core of hard substance, a three dimensional quality, a feeling of solidity, and luminous precision of structure and image. We can illustrate these qualities in such lines as,

> No handiwork of Callimachus,
> Who handled marble as if it were bronze,
> Made draperies that seemed to rise
> When sea-wind swept the corner, stands;
> His long lamp-chimney shaped like the stem
> Of a slender palm, stood but a day[100]

or in the lines,

Here at right of the entrance this bronze head,
Human, superhuman, a bird's round eye,
Everything else withered and mummy-dead.[101]

or in,

World-famous golden-thighed Pythagoras
Fingered upon a fiddle-stick or strings
What a star sang and careless Muses heard:
Old clothes upon old sticks to scare a bird.[102]

Thus we can see the stylistic development of Yeats as a parallel to the development of his idea of the craftsman as his model. His feeling for objectivity and clarity, and his intuition of art as a symbol of the supernatural find their full expression in sculpture and metal work or carving. Therefore ideas of design, structure, measurement and form replace the early fanciful romantic yearnings for a never never land of fairy twilight. His style too accompanies this change of emphasis from the vaguely romantic to the precision of works of art in its greater distinctness and sharper edge. Thus the early poetical dreamy Yeats outgrows himself by putting on the mask of a deliberate craftsman.

Yeats's exaltation of the craftsman reflects a new appreciation of the craftsman's life and work during the late Victorian period. Thanks to Ruskin's lyrical praise of the medieval craftsman contrasting his freedom and creativity with the drudgery of the modern debased industrial worker, the high aesthetic value put on the products of his skill and the attempts to revive the beauty of the crafts by William Morris, and the great Exhibition of Paris where for the first time the wealth and quality of Oriental crafts were displayed before European observers, the words "crafts," and "handicraftsman" acquired a new significant connotation, carrying with them the suggestion of vast imaginative wealth and traditional delicacy of skill at work on the great religious symbols of medieval Europe or ancient Greece or the Eastern cultures. This is the cultural background against which Yeats continues to explore and imitate the life and work of the traditional craftsman.

CHAPTER II

# THE IDEA OF THE POETIC WORD

An important aspect of the "craft of verse" in Yeats's poetry is his constant experiment in the use of words in order to charge them with meanings peculiar to him. Like all poets he wrestles with words in his effort to make poetic language a means of exploring and communicating an inner reality. Ordinarily language is a social or impersonal medium in which words have primarily a denotative surface. Every poet has to transmute it so that the denotative meaning yields to a connotative power conveying the full context of his thought, feeling and mood. In the case of mystical or visionary poets like Yeats the usual meaning in common usage yields to an esoteric one which, like his symbols, can be comprehended only by a careful observation and analysis of his idiom in diverse contexts, and by a comparison of its functions in them for arriving at its meaning below the surface.

Because of his life-long preoccupation with style it is in the fitness of things that the first poem in Yeats's *Collected Poems* should deal with an affirmation of his faith in the potency of the word. His faith recalls the Biblical idea of the Word that existed before it was made flesh, or the analogous Hindu mystical belief that all creation is a resonance of the primordial sound "Aum." "Words alone are certain good," says Yeats, and goes on to dwell on this mystery:

> The wandering earth herself may be
> Only a sudden flaming word,
> In clanging space a moment heard,
> Troubling the endless reverie.[1]

With this sense of the creative power of the Word in the beginning Yeats combines a faith in the immortality of the words of a song.

The words of common speech attain in a poet's art a higher existence; Yeats compares them to oysters dying into pearls:

> Go gather by the humming sea
> Some twisted, echo-harbouring shell,
> And to its lips thy story tell,
> And they thy comforters will be,
> Rewording in melodious guile
> Thy fretful words a little while,
> Till they shall singing fade in ruth
> And die a pearly brotherhood;
> For words alone are certain good:
> Sing, then, for this is also sooth.

In several of Yeats's pronouncements on the use of language in poetry there is always the reference to this feeling of something occult or magical about words. The commonplace phrase which speaks of the "magic of words" has almost a literal truth for him:

> Have not poetry and music arisen, as it seems, out of the sounds the enchanters made to help their imagination to enchant, to charm, to bind with a spell themselves and the passers-by? These very words, a chief part of all praises of music or poetry, still cry to us their origin. (1901)[2]

This occult power of words is exploited by men of imagination to hypnotize their listeners. To restore this lost link between magic and poetic speech, poets must return to the ways of their predecessors in the remote past at the very source of all poetry:

> It is not until they have been forced to use their imagination and express the inmost meaning of the words, not until their thought imposes itself upon all listeners and each word invokes a special mode of beauty, that the method rises once more from the dead and becomes a living art.
>
> It is the belief in the power of words and the delight in the purity of sound that will make the arts of plain chant and recitative the great arts they are described as being by those who first practised them. (1901)[3]

Yeats cites the example of the blind poet Raftery whose words cast such a spell on his listeners that the "peasant girl commended by song" became a magical presence to them and made them pursue her:

And certain men, being maddened by those rhymes,
Or else by toasting her a score of times,
Rose from the table and declared it right
To test their fancy by their sight;
But they mistook the brightness of the moon
For the prosaic light of day—
Music had driven their wits astray—
And one was drowned in the great bog of Cloone. (1928)[4]

Like that "beauty's blind rambling celebrant,"[5] Yeats too wants to hypnotize his reader:

O may the moon and sunlight seem
One inextricable beam,
For if I triumph I must make men mad.[6]

The thought recalls Coleridge's nostalgic desire for the power of the Abyssinian maid's song so that he could "build that dome in air" and "those caves of ice" and "all who heard should see them there."[7]

This return to the source of power in imaginative writing is possible, according to Yeats, only by the rejection of all externality on which declamation or picturesque description is based.[8] For him this has been the influence of the scientific movement on literature in reaction against which the French symbolist writers began to dwell upon the element of evocation and suggestion in poetry. He must take "rhetoric and wring its neck" before he can achieve a style of his own in which words will have some flame-like incandescence.[9] He recognizes his quest of a new style as part of a larger movement of the mind of Europe impelled by the same time-spirit:

I did not then understand that the change was from beyond my own mind, . . . writers are struggling all over Europe . . . against that picturesque and declamatory way of writing, against that 'externality' which a time of scientific and political thought has brought into literature . . . Count Villiers de L'Isle-Adam swept together, by what seemed a sudden energy, words behind which glimmered a spiritual and passionate mood, as the flame glimmers behind the dusky blue and red glass in an Eastern lamp; and created persons from whom has fallen all even of personal characteristic except a thirst for that hour when all things shall pass like a cloud. . . . (1898)[10]

In making language a vehicle of mystical or visionary experience of the spirit, the Symbolist poets are practicing a theory of suggestion in poetry known in traditional Oriental poetics as "dhvani" meaning resonance. Anandavardhana, a tenth century Sanskrit critic, in a famous work, *Dhvanyaloka* says:

> That kind of poetry, wherein either the (conventional) word renders itself or its meaning secondary, (respectively), and suggests the implied meaning is designated by the learned as DHVANI or "suggestive poetry."[11]

It is not unlikely that the Symbolist theory of suggestion and poetic language was influenced by the movement of transcendental thought that swept over Europe and America in the nineteenth century. It may be recalled that Symbolism has been an integral part of Indian poetics; speech according to *The Upanishads* corresponds to fire among the elements. Mallarmé's ideal of the new poetic language is akin to the Indian theory of *Dhvani* or resonance:

> That we are now precisely at the moment of seeking, before that breaking up of large rhythms of literature and their scattering in articulate, almost instrumental, nervous waves, an art which shall complete the transposition, into the Book, of the symphony, or simply recapture our own: for, it is in elementary sonorities of brass, strings, wood, unquestionably, but in the intellectual word at its utmost, that, fully and evidently, we should find, drawing to itself all the correspondences of the universe, the supreme Music.[12]

Yeats's comparison of words glimmering with a spiritual and passionate mood to "the flame behind the dusky blue and red glass in an Eastern lamp" is typical because it likens a poet's craft in words to that of stained glass. His favorite metaphor for words in poetry is drawn from flame or fire or light: words "take light from mutual reflection, like an actual trail of fire over precious stones."[13] The phrasing and the thought are a verbatim repetition of Mallarmé's statement:

> "The pure work . . . implies the elocutionary disappearance of the poet, who yields place to the words, immobilised by the shock of their inequality; they take light from mutual reflection, like an actual trail of fire over precious stones, replacing the old lyric afflatus or the enthusiastic personal direction of the phrase." "The verse which out of many vocables remakes an entire word, new, unknown to the language, and as if magical, attains this isolation of speech."[14]

Quoting Saint-Beauve, Yeats elsewhere says that style is the only immortal thing in literature; the image of a fire transfiguring words, and the secret of craftsmanship recur. It is the product of a still unexpended energy after all that the story and argument needs,

> a still unbroken pleasure after the immediate end has been accomplished—to build this up into a most personal and wilful fire, transfiguring words and sounds and events. It is the playing of strength when the day's work is done, a secret between a craftsman and his craft, and is so inseparate in his nature that he has it most of all amid overwhelming emotion, and in the face of death.[15]

These general ideas of Yeats as to the manner in which words function in poetry are illustrated by his practice in the composition of his poems. By various devices he succeeds in shaping an idiom in which words acquire something of this fire, light or resonance of which he speaks. The words that acquire a special luminous quality by their "mutual reflection" and "form a trail of fire over precious stones" do so by a craftsmanship carefully arranging them in diverse contexts, by the repetition of certain clusters of words in several poems, and by habitual association with some of his principal themes. These words can be called complex because through repeated association they carry special meanings in his work as distinguished from the general meanings they have in common usage.

Like all poets Yeats has his own idiom,[16] and the tendency to repeat his favorite words and phrases. With every repetition they gather fresh associations from earlier contexts, and a structure of meaning is built up in them through this process. Empson describes these words as "complex words" in poetry.[17] Yeats uses complex words for linking up the poems within a section so as to unify them. The poems are unified not only in terms of themes, experiences, images and symbols; they are also unified by the deliberate craft of repeating significant words and carrying them forward from poem to poem. Furthermore these words and phrases are carried over from one book of poems to the next making them the links in a continuous chain of evolution. This is one of the methods Yeats employs to reach his ideal of the unity of a book reflecting the unity of being.

Such complex words in Yeats can be classified into the four following kinds:

1. There are words in his work which by repetition gather special meanings or suggestions in his poems. The context for these special meanings is the whole corpus of Yeats. Some of these words are grouped together in clusters in some poems. The context for these is a group of poems.
2. There are a large number of compound epithets scattered all over his work which are peculiar to him as a kind of short-hand code to express his meaning. These compound epithets are also an integral part of his craft of words.
3. Yeats also uses proper names (predominantly Irish) of places and persons from history, fiction and autobiography so as to make them symbolic like names in mythology. These proper names also acquire complexity of meaning.
4. His poems have an allusive technique by which certain traditional key words are re-echoed from literary masterpieces of the past, and a recognition of this allusiveness is absolutely vital to our response to the meaning of the poem. Verbal complexity of this allusive type employed for the revival or suggestion of older modes of consciousness can be viewed as an instrument for inducing what Owen Barfield terms as "change of consciousness."[18]

A careful reading of Yeats's poems reveals his use of these four kinds of complexity in his handling of words. The next two chapters will explore this subject in greater detail.

CHAPTER III

# COMPLEX WORDS AND COMPOUND EPITHETS

FIRST, the device of enriching the connotation of a word by repetition in various contexts and by association with other words—by what Yeats calls "mutual reflection" of their light—is illustrated by his use of the word "moon."[1] Through the greater part of his work written over a period of thirty years we can watch him creating his own special meanings conveyed by this word. The moon is often associated in his early poetry with a world of transience:

> '. . . God shall come from the sea with a sigh
> And bid the stars drop down from the sky,
> And the moon like a pale rose wither away.'
> Book I. ll.425–427. (1889)[2]

Death and ruin, sea and moon are again brought together in close association in this passage:

> 'I hear my soul drop down into decay,
> And Manannan's dark tower, stone after stone,
> Gather sea-slime and fall the seaward way,
> And the moon goad the waters night and day,
> That all be overthrown.
> Book II. ll.235–239.

Soul, star and moon are associated in the draft lines,

> The soul is a drop of joy afar.
> In other years from some old star
> It fell, or from the twisted moon
> Dripped on the earth.
> Book I. ll.276–279.

In the final version the lines become:

> 'Men's hearts of old were drops of flame
> That from the saffron morning came,
> Or drops of silver joy that fell
> Out of the moon's pale twisted shell.
> Book I. ll.276–279

The same cluster of associations of ideas of decay and death with the moon and shell and stars recurs in 'Adam's Curse':

> We sat grown quiet at the name of love;
> We saw the last embers of daylight die,
> And in the trembling blue-green of the sky
> A moon, worn as if it had been a shell
> Washed by time's waters as they rose and fell
> About the stars and broke in days and years. (1902)

The poem as it significantly ends on the word "moon" gathers in its last lines the suggestions of decay and emptiness in the human world, ". . . it had all seemed happy, and yet we'd grown / As weary-hearted as the hollow moon."

From such early repetitive nucleus of associations augmented by his reading in Eastern religions and Theosophy, Yeats builds up his myth of the cycles of birth and rebirth in *A Vision*. In this myth the moon is the presiding power over generation and decay. We have an anticipation of the idea in the lines,

> The Pestle of the Moon
> That pounds up all anew
> Brings me to birth again. (1914)[3]

'The Phases of the Moon' (1918) is a verse summary of *A Vision*. 'The Cat and the Moon' (1917) dwells on the myth, "The pure cold light in the sky / Troubled his animal blood." The process of the world follows the changes of the moon:

> Does Minnaloushe know that his pupils
> Will pass from change to change,
> And that from round to crescent,
> From crescent to round they range?
> Minnaloushe creeps through the grass

Alone, important and wise,
And lifts to the changing moon
His changing eyes.

While Minnaloushe is unconscious of this influence though subject to it, the wise Solomon can interpret to the Witch the nature of her experience when she lies in his arms "under the wild moon." The thought of the "frenzy of the fourteenth moon" when "The soul begins to tremble into stillness, / To die into the labyrinth of itself!"[4] is recalled in the lines, "Therefore a blessed moon last night / Gave Sheba to her Solomon," (1918)[5] and in the conclusion of the poem, "And the moon is wilder every minute. / O! Solomon! let us try again."[6]

As Yeats's rage against the destruction of beautiful things and against old age becomes intense, his epithets for the moon are indicative of this destructive power:

> Many ingenious lovely things are gone
> That seemed sheer miracle to the multitude,
> Protected from the circle of the moon
> That pitches common things about. (1922)[7]

The draft line for the above "the murderous treachery of the moon / Or all that wayward ebb and flow . . ."[8] recalls a similar phrase in 'A Prayer for My Daughter' "the murderous innocence of the sea."

The words "blood" and "bloody" carry the same connotation in their association with the moon. The title of a poem 'Blood and the Moon' is a typical Yeatsian juxtaposition of two words which have acquired special private meanings in his idiom. The phrases, "this winding, gyring, spiring treadmill of a stair," "sybilline frenzy blind," "blood-sodden breast," "all things" are "a dream," culminate in the thought of the world as "pragmatical, preposterous pig of a world, its farrow that so solid seem / Must vanish on the instant if the mind but change its theme." It is a world where "everything that is not God" must be "consumed with intellectual fire." The third section of the poem groups together these complex clusters of words. A lunatic world in its murderous moon-struck bloodshed and the "purity" of the moon are yoked together with a violence of association peculiar to Yeats: "purity," "unclouded moon," "pure," "innocence," on the one hand and "arrowy shaft," "blood," (repeated four times in twelve lines) "stain," "soldier," "assassin," "executioner," "drunken frenzy" on the other clearly illustrate the technique of Yeats in building up complex meanings by association and contrast and by recapturing earlier usage in his poems of these words. In 'Blood and the Moon,' the word moon is used to suggest the paradox of murderous innocence. The moon itself remains in inviolable purity while the world in its moon-struck frenzy is violent:

> The purity of the unclouded moon
> Has flung its arrowy shaft upon the floor.
> Seven centuries have passed and it is pure,
> The blood of innocence has left no stain.
> There, on blood-saturated ground, have stood
> Soldier, assassin, executioner,
> Whether for daily pittance or in blind fear
> Or out of abstract hatred, and shed blood,
> But could not cast a single jet thereon.
> Odour of blood on the ancestral stair!
> And we that have shed none must gather there
> And clamour in drunken frenzy for the moon. (1928)

Wisdom which can rise above this lunar determinism is the property of the dead, "a something incompatible with life";

> . . . and power,
> Like everything that has the stain of blood,
> A property of the living; but no stain
> Can come upon the visage of the moon
> When it has looked in glory from a cloud.

'Blood and the Moon' was probably composed in 1928, and it is followed the next year by another poem on an allied theme with another Yeatsian title, 'The Crazed Moon.' Yeats's earlier romantic words like "sea," "star" and "shell" used in association with the moon now yield place to a more realistic tone: "craze," "crazy" are words frequently used by the later Yeats, and the poem has a characteristic opening:

> Crazed through much child-bearing
> The moon is staggering in the sky;

> Moon-struck by the despairing
> Glances of her wandering eye
> We grope, and grope in vain,
> For children born of her pain.

At her height in her "virginal pride" the world has been moved to a dance under her influence; the idea recalls that of the 'Cat and the Moon,' "Do you dance, Minnaloushe, do you dance?" The bitter end of this process of generation in decay is the theme of the third stanza:

> Fly-catchers of the moon,
> Our hands are blenched, our fingers seem
> But slender needles of bone;
> Blenched by that malicious dream
> They are spread wide that each
> May rend what comes in reach.

As Yeats writes of the transitory nature of the world thus subject to the changes of the moon, the words "bitter," "violent," "frenzy," "fury" are frequently repeated in his poems. As Niamh descends from eternity to time, she is questioned, "What dream came with you that you came / Through bitter tide on foam-wet feet?"[9] Cuchulain battled with the "bitter tide." Times "bitter flood,"[10] "Love's bitter mystery,"[11] "the bitter glass,"[12] "bitter bread"[13] are typical examples. Yeats's dialectical thinking leads him to attribute man's wisdom and art to their origin in or as antithetical to this bitterness. Out of the perishing illusions of this world man's visions are born. The words "wise," "wisdom," "beauty," "sweetness" are often associated thus with the word "bitter" or "bitterness," as in the following examples:

> For He who made you bitter made you wise.[14]

> Plucked bitter wisdom that enriched his blood.[15]

> Bitter sweetness of the night.[16]

> O bitter reward / Of many a tragic tomb.[17]

> Beauty that we have won / From bitterest hours.[18]

Out of their bitterness some violent or angry men create great works of art:

> Some violent bitter man, some powerful man
> Called architect and artist in, that they,
> Bitter and violent men, might rear in stone
> The sweetness that all longed for night and day,
> The gentleness none there had ever known. (1923)[19]

All art takes its origin in these roots of bitterness or violence:

> O what if gardens where the peacock strays
> With delicate feet upon old terraces,
> Or else all Juno from an urn displays
> Before the indifferent garden deities;
> O what if levelled lawns and gravelled ways
> Where slippered Contemplation finds his ease
> And Childhood a delight for every sense,
> But take our greatness with our violence?[20]

If wisdom, sweetness and greatness are all born of bitterness, man's entire world is also a product of this experience:

> Death and life were not
> Till man made up the whole,
> Made lock, stock and barrel
> Out of his bitter soul,
> Aye, sun and moon and star, all. (1927)[21]

It is this same bitter soul that makes him create the opposite of his temporal world in eternity—his "translunar Paradise."

The journey of the soul from this bitter world to the beyond is the theme of 'Byzantium.' Almost every significant word or phrase in the poem has a complexity of meaning intelligible only in the context of Yeats's use of the same word or phrase elsewhere in his work. The fuller our memory of these words elsewhere the richer their meaning in the poem. Oisin's cloak is "dim with the mire of a mortal shore."[22] The body of the dead Adonis is "that thing all blood and mire, that beast-torn wreck."[23] The words are grouped together again in the question in 'The Gyres,' "What matter though numb nightmare ride on top, / And blood and mire the sensitive body stain?" These words together with the phrase "moon embittered" are all brought together so as to intensify or light up each other's meaning by mutual reflection in the lines:

> Or, by the moon embittered, scorn aloud
> In glory of changeless metal
> Common bird or petal
> And all complexities of mire or blood.

Again as the poem ends the oft-repeated words are juxtaposed with meanings enriched by association with other contexts:

> Astraddle on the dolphin's mire and blood,
> Spirit after spirit! The smithies break the flood,
> The golden smithies of the Emperor!
> Marbles of the dancing floor
> Break bitter furies of complexity.

If the words "bitter," "blood" and "mire" connote Yeats's associations with the world of time, "flame" and "fire" suggest the world of eternity or transcendence. "God's fire,"[24] "until God burn Nature with a kiss,"[25] "Look on that fire, salvation walks within,"[26] are some characteristic expressions. For supernatural spirits, the word "flame" is almost invariably used; here are some examples: "wing above wing, flame above flame,"[27] "the ghastly ghost flames,"[28] "My soul shall touch with his and the two flames . . ."[29] "Our souls shall warm their loves at many a rustling flame,"[30] and "embattled flaming multitude."[31] 'Byzantium' (1929) describes the process of spirit creation out of the world of bitterness and complexity in the same language:

> At midnight on the Emperor's pavement flit
> Flames that no faggot feeds, nor steel has lit,
> Nor storm disturbs, flames begotten of flame,
> Where blood-begotten spirits come
> And all complexities of fury leave,
> Dying into a dance,
> An agony of trance,
> An agony of flame that cannot singe a sleeve.

The soul journeys from the bitter world of the moon and blood to the flames of the spiritual world. In this journey it passes through the phase of "tragic gaiety" born of wisdom and insight.

Like the word "bitter" for earthly experience, the words "gay" and "gaiety" are often used to connote this state of mystic joy. Corresponding to the journey of the soul through these three stages—blood and mire, tragic gaiety, and spiritual illumination—Yeats's entire work can be categorized into three divisions, reminiscent of Keats's well-known comparison of life to a mansion of three apartments of maiden thought, suffering, and soul-making. In the first part of his work we have the adolescent dreamer or idealist nursing the hope of joy in the world of earthly fulfillment. The second is the dawning of maturity when all desire and beauty become a bitter torment. The third deals with the theme of tragic joy and the wisdom that enables the soul to grow from bitterness into the gaiety of the tragic hero, "Gaiety transfiguring all that dread".[32]

The progressive use of the word "gay" from the early poems to the last indicates the growing complexity it acquires through repetition in significant contexts. The fairy people, says the early 'Faery Song,' (1891) are "old and gay." Laughter and gaiety are associated with God in a manner reminiscent of pagan and Hindu Gods:

> God's laughing in Heaven
> To see you so good;
> The Sailing Seven
> Are gay with His mood. (1890)[33]

O'Driscoll is a dreamer and a singer: "And never was piping so sad, / And never was piping so gay."[34] The maker of the peacock will be gay in eternity as in time:

> His ghost will be gay
> Adding feather to feather
> For the pride of his eye. (1914)

The thought recalls that of 'The Indian upon God' (1886) "Who made the grass and made the worms and made my feathers gay." 'Oedipus at Colonus' (1927) is an anticipation of the mood of the last poems where the tragic hero's death is a "bridal chamber of joy." "The bride is carried to the bridegroom's chamber through torchlight and tumultuous song; / I celebrate the silent kiss that ends short life or long." "Never to have lived is best," . . ."The second best's a gay goodnight and quickly turn away." 'Lapis Lazuli' is a defense of the gaiety of the artist and the visionary against the complaint of hysterical women who are sick of "poets that are always gay." All the world is a stage, and the drama of eternity is being played on it. There is nothing here for tears, it is all gay with vision and joy, ". . . Hamlet and Lear are gay; / Gaiety transfiguring all that dread." Civilizations come and go, and beautiful things are made and destroyed. In the midst of all this destruction the redeemed soul of the contemplative Chinese sage is full of joy, "All things fall and are built again, / And those that build them again are gay." The Chinamen look upon this scene of recurrent transcience from their serene lofty height, "Their eyes mid many wrinkles, their eyes, / Their ancient, glittering eyes, are gay."

The word "gay" used in his early poems for the fairy world now acquires new depth suggesting tragic joy and wisdom. It has grown through three levels of meaning by repetition in three distinguishable contexts. At first it is used somewhat conventionally in connection with Celtic folklore and the fairy world.[35] Its connotation deepens to connote the experience of Greek and Shakespearean tragedy. It reaches its deepest level of meaning in the last poems like 'Lapis Lazuli' to suggest Oriental transcendental wisdom and its vision above the cycles of time.

The words "moon," "bitter," "flame" and "gay" acquiring special meanings through repetition in diverse contexts in Yeats's work are examples of his deliberate craft of words charging them with uncommon suggestive power. They grow individually as they recur in his poems and give them their continuity. They also appear together in clusters in various contexts and augment each other's meaning by their juxtaposition. These complex words and word clusters become a shuttle weaving his entire work into a single web.

## II

Another significant aspect of Yeats's craft of words for achieving complexity in poetic idiom is the making of numerous compound epithets. Like Spenser, Shakespeare, Milton, Shelley and Keats, he has a high frequency of such compounds. Very often in the early poems there are echoes of compound epithets from other poets. "Fever-free," ('The Madness of King Goll,' *Variorum* ed.), and "vapour-turbaned steep," ('The Man Who Dreamed of Faeryland'), recall Shakespeare's compounds "fancy-free" (*Midsummer Night's Dream*, II.i.166), and "cloud-capped towers" (*The Tempest* IV.i.153). "Sweet-throated like a bird"[36] ('Cuchulain's Fight with the Sea'), "dew-dropping hours"[37] ('A Faery Song'), "wine-stained"[38] ('The Secret Rose'), and "death-pale"[39] ('The Travail of Passion'), have a Keatsian ring. Most of the epithets in the early poems are somewhat in the Romantic idiom of Pre-Raphaelite poetry like "echo-harbouring shell" ('The Song of the Happy Shepherd'), "silver-sandalled" ('To the Rose upon the Rood of Time'), "thought-woven sails" ('The Rose of Battle'), "world-forgotten isle" ('A Man Who Dreamed of Faeryland'), "bee-loud glade" ('Lake Isle of Innisfree'), "rose-breath" ('To the Rose upon the Rood of Time'), "red-rose bordered hem" ('To Ireland in the Coming Times'), "Passion-dimmed eyes" ('He Reproves the Curlew'), "silver-shoed / Pale silver-proud queen-woman of the sky" ('The Ragged Wood').

There are many examples of this kind of epithets which are dreamy and remote in quality in Yeats's early poetry. Particularly typical of this phase are compounds formed with "dream" like "dream-heavy hour," "dream-heavy land" ('He Remembers Forgotten Beauty'), "dream-dimmed eyes" ('He Tells of a Valley Full of Lovers'), "dream-awakened eyes" ('The Valley of the Black Pig'). Likewise he is fond of compounds formed with the epithet "pale" like "cloud-pale eyelids" ('He Tells of a Valley Full of Lovers'), "pearl-pale" ('He Gives His Beloved Certain Rhymes'), "milk-pale" ('Wanderings of Oisin,' Bk.II.l.134), "honey-pale" ('The Withering of the Boughs'). Another frequent series of such compounds is formed with the word "dew" like "love-dew" ('Wanderings of Oisin,' Bk.III.l.424), "dew-blanched horns" ('Wanderings of Oisin,' Bk.III.l.30), "dew-dabbled" ('The White Birds'), "dew-dropping hours" ('A Faery Song'), and "dew-cold lilies" ('He Remembers Forgotten Beauty').

Yeats turns away from such compounds in the conventional poetical idiom of the late Victorian period to compound epithets like "that dolphin-torn, that gong-tormented sea" ('Byzantium') with their explosive power; it is easy to perceive the change in his coinage and use of such compounds. The early epithets are pictorial, sensuous and diffuse. On the other hand the later ones are fresh, packed with Yeatsian meanings of a complex nature, and entirely characteristic of his imagination and phrasing. "Moon-accursed" ('Man Young and Old'), and "moon-struck" ('The Crazed Moon'), are compounds that carry the usual complex meanings he associates with the word "moon." Equally significant are the compounds with "blood" as the base in "blood-dimmed tide" ('The Second Coming'), "blood-sodden breast" ('Blood and the Moon'), "blood-begotten spirits" ('Byzantium'), "blood-sodden heart" ('Vacillation vi'), "blood-bedabbled breast" ('Her Vision in the Wood'), and "blood-saturated ground" ('Blood and the Moon'). The words "wind" and "storm" almost always have symbolic or supernatural connotation in Yeats, and there are numerous compounds with these as the base: "wind-blown reed" ('Fergus and the Druid'), "wind-blown flame" ('The Lover Asks Forgiveness Because of His Many Moods'), "wind-blown clamour" ('Beggar to Beggar Cried'), "wind-beaten tower" ('Ego Dominus Tuus'), "storm-broken trees" ('In Memory of Major Robert Gregory'), "storm-beaten breast" ('On a Political Prisoner'), "storm-beaten old watch-tower" ('Symbols'), and "storm-scattered intricacy" ('Vacillation'). An even longer compound of the same kind is "haystack-and roof-levelling wind" ('A Prayer for My Daughter').

Compound epithets have always the effect of compression, and Yeats's later style becomes condensed almost to the point of obscurity. He loads his lines with these compounds, often using more than one in the same line: "rock-born, rock-wandering foot" ('The Grey Rock'), "rock-bred, sea-borne" ('On a Political Prisoner'), "death-in-life and life-in-death" ('Byzantium'), echoing Coleridge, "that dolphin-torn, that gong-tormented sea" ('Byzantium'), "rage-driven, rage-tormented, and rage-hungry troop" ('I See Phantoms of Hatred and of the Heart's Fullness and of the Coming Emptiness'), "Camel-back, horse-back, ass-back, mule-back" ('Lapis Lazuli'), are examples of lines weighted with heavy compounds carrying complex suggestions.

Because of Yeats's view of the ultimate reality of the inner self or soul of man, it is only natural that he should use a number of compounds emphasizing the inner reality of man's self like "self-born" ('Among School Children'), "self-delighting, self-appeasing, self-affrighting" ('A Prayer for My Daughter'), and "self-sown, self-begotten" ('Colonus's Praise'). The word "self" in these contexts has the same significance as the word *atman* in *The Upanishads* which Yeats translated with Swami Purohit Swami. The external world which opposes this inner self is often the theme of Yeats, and typical of his Buddhistic contempt or disgust for the world of the flesh or illusion are phrases like "frog-spawn" ('A Dialogue of Self and Soul'), "mirror-scaled serpent is multiplicity" ('Ribh Denounces Patrick'), "rag-and-bone shop of the heart" ('The Circus Animal's Desertion'). These are Oriental in their suggestion.

Such compound epithets as these are new in English poetry. From the time of Homer, compounds have always been used by poets. But like Homer's "rosy-fingered morn," or "wine-dark sea," or old English kennings like "famigheals" (foamy-necked) or Shakespeare's "heaven-kissing hill" or Keats's "purple-stained mouth" they have had a decorative or pictorial function in poetry. But in Yeats's typical compounds we have a certain complexity of symbolic or abstract meaning that can be decoded only in terms of his thought or philosophy. These compounds are a kind of shorthand for his quick and suggestive expression. "Plummet-measured face" ('The Statues'), "great-rooted blossomer" ('Among School Children'), "mirror-resembling dream" ('The Tower'), or "mackerel-crowded seas" ('Sailing to Byzantium'), and "self-delighting reverie" ('I See Phantoms of Hatred and of the Heart's Fullness and of the Coming Emptiness'), yield their full meanings only to the reader familiar with Yeats's philosophy and his peculiarities of phrase. In the sense that these phrases are charged with implications peculiar to him, we can describe them as complex.

CHAPTER IV

# VERBAL ALLUSIVENESS AND MEANING

JUST AS HE USES COMMON NOUNS and adjectives in a complex manner Yeats also employs several proper names in senses somewhat peculiar to him. These are not only the names of mythical places or persons, but those of historical persons and fictional characters. The Buddha, Pythagoras, Plato, Plotinus, Phidias, Michelangelo, Blake, Shelley and Swift belong to the former category; Lear, Hamlet, Timon, Cordelia and Ophelia are taken from the world of fiction. By fusing these together Yeats deepens their connotation or their suggestiveness.

The process by which these names become complex in the ideas they suggest can be illustrated with reference to 'The Statues.' The names that Yeats associates together in the poem are Pythagoras, Phidias, the Buddha, Hamlet, Pearse and Cuchulain. The poem is admittedly obscure, and it has therefore elicited a great deal of critical comment and analysis. The obscurity arises because the poem is a highly condensed expression of Yeats's interpretation of sculptures both Eastern and Western in different periods of history. It traces the story of art from the beginning to the present, contrasting the present with the past. Underlying the poem is the theme that the sculptures represent the ideal human form, and that the ideal human form is ultimately the embodiment of the soul. The thought behind these sculptures is the thought of Spenser in the lines, "For of the soule the bodie forme doth take: / For soule is forme, and doth the bodie make."[1] or Blake's idea that the body is that part of the soul which we can see with the naked eye. It is against this philosophy of form as a spiritual symbol that we should read the poem. The proper names used in it add their suggestiveness to this argument. Pythagoras supplied the mathematical basis for the sculptor's plummet. His "numbers" are specifically mentioned. But it may also be recalled that Pythagoras according to tradition is associated with the belief in the transmigration of the soul. It is this that makes him a bridge between the Western world and the East whence this idea was absorbed by him. Yeats has already referred to Pythagoras' knowledge of music 'Among School Children':

> World-famous golden-thighed Pythagoras
> Fingered upon a fiddle stick or strings,
> What a star sang and careless Muses heard.

Commenting on this, Yeats writes to Olivia Shakespear, "Pythagoras made some measurement of the intervals between notes on a stretched string."[2] Thus Pythagorean number, music and his belief in the soul as the source of these symbols are associated in Yeats's mind. The invisible and the visible thus come together in him first. In Phidias this fusion reaches its finest visible perfection as the gods are endowed with the idealized human form in his sculptures. Yeats's poem moves between the East and the West or between the philosophy of the former and the art of the latter. While the abstract idea of the soul's transmigration travelled through Pythagoras to the West, the concrete embodiment of the divine in Phidias now travels to the East in the fusion of Apollo and the Buddha in Gandhara sculpture. Ancient Persian religion and Buddhism prohibited the representation of the divine in statues. Hindu art portrayed the gods in superhuman "many-headed" forms. According to Yeats's the defeat of such "Asiatic vague immensities" was brought about not by the battle at Salamis, but by Greek artists who surpassed Pythagoras because they embodied his calculations in statues "that look but casual flesh."

The opening argument of the 'Statues' is built around these Yeatsian associations with the names of Pythagoras, Phidias, Apollo and the Buddha. From the thought of the Buddha, Yeats proceeds to recall Hamlet. Both the Buddha and Hamlet share the same physical form and the same spiritual vision. Both are fat, philosophical princes; both despise the outer world and return to the inner. Yeats's drafts of the poem show that the experience of the "emptiness" of the world was shared by the Buddha and Hamlet.[3]

Gandhara (4th century): Buddha

Gupta Art (Mathura, India, 5th–6th century): Buddha

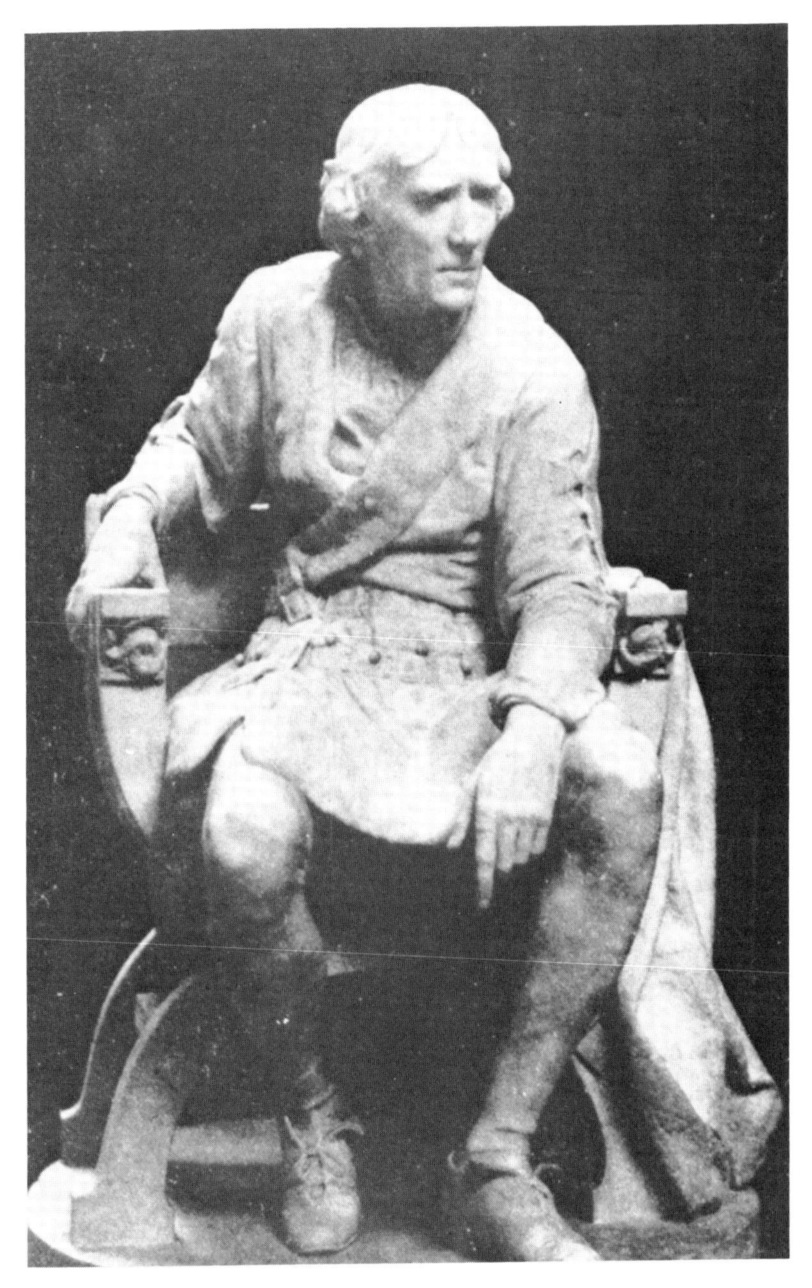

Irving as Hamlet
From the statue in the Guildhall by E. Onslow Ford, R.A.

G. F. Watts' William Morris
(Courtesy: National Portrait Gallery, London)

It is not unlikely that he has a vivid image of the "form" of Hamlet as that of the Renaissance man from Ophelia's description of him as the "glass of fashion, and the mould of form . . . That unmatched form and feature of blown youth . . . The expectancy and rose of the state." Yeats probably also recalls Hamlet's praise of his father in terms of sculpture comparing him to Greek statues of Hercules, Hyperion, Jove, Mars and Mercury. He may also have considered Hamlet's praise of man as corresponding to Greek statuary:

What a piece of work is man! how noble in reason! how infinite in faculty! in form and moving how express and admirable! in action how like an angel! in apprehension how like a god! the beauty of the world, the paragon of animals!

The Hamlet that Yeats associates with the Buddha is not the "thin" Hamlet of popular conception, but the "fat" Hamlet of Shakespeare as the Renaissance man, and his vivid recollection of Henry Irving playing the role. Yeats's association of ideas connecting Hamlet and the Buddha can be seen from his comment on a portrait of William Morris in *Autobiographies*:

A reproduction of his portrait by Watts hangs over my mantlepiece with Henley's, and those of other friends. Its grave wide-open eyes, like the eyes of some dreaming beast, remind me of the open eyes of Titian's 'Ariosto', while the broad vigorous body suggests a mind that has no need of the intellect to remain sane, though it gave itself to every phantasy: the dreamer of the Middle Ages. It is 'the fool of faery . . . wide and wild as a hill', the resolute European image that yet half remembers Buddha's motionless meditation, and has no trait in common with the wavering lean image of hungry speculation, that cannot but because of certain famous Hamlets of our stage fill the mind's eye. Shakespeare himself foreshadowed a symbolic change, that is, a change in the whole temperament of the world, for though he called his Hamlet 'fat' and even 'scant of breath,' he thrust between his fingers agile rapier and dagger.[4]

"Golden-thighed" Pythagoras, Phidias' Apollo, Eastern sculptures of the Buddha, Shakespeare's Hamlet and Watts's William Morris are symbols of the same soul reincarnating itself in the perfection of human form in diverse times and cultures. A later example in this chain of successive incarnations is the spirit of Cuchulain entering Pearse when the latter summoned him to his side at the Easter Rising. Yeats is here alluding to the statue of Cuchulain erected as a memorial to the executed leaders of the rebellion. This belief in the occult perpetual life of the soul is the "ancient sect" of Ireland to which Yeats alludes in 'Under Ben Bulben':

> Many times man lives and dies
> Between two eternities,
> That of race and that of soul.

From the "formless spawning fury" of degenerate modern art, Yeats wants men to return to a sense of traditional form or measurement as symbolic of the world of the soul. This belief is "our proper dark,"—a mysterious cult—and it is only when men climb back to it that they can again "trace / The lineaments of a plummet-measured face." In Yeats's mind the belief in the soul and artistic expression grow and decline together.

The influence of Pater on the thought of the poem has been traced in detail by Engelberg.[5] It seems probable that the poem draws upon Yeats's recollections of Pater's sensitive response to La Gioconda of Da Vinci. As in these statues so too in Da Vinci's painting according to Pater the "ends of the world are come," and the "eyelids are a little weary." Their beauty is from within: "It is beauty wrought out from within upon the flesh, the deposit, little cell by cell, of strange thoughts, and fantastic reveries and exquisite passions. . . ."[6] All the cultures of the world reach their culmination in one ideal form embodying the perpetual life of the reincarnating soul:

> All the thoughts and experience of the world have etched and moulded there, in that which they have of power to refine and make expressive the outward form, the animalism of Greece, the lust of Rome, the mysticism of the middle age with its spiritual ambition and imaginative loves, the return of the Pagan world, the sins of the Borgias.[7]

As Yeats follows the same pattern of thought in tracing the fusion of cultures in the statues, he also recalls the world of the soul and its transmigration through birth and death in Pater's description of Mona Lisa. This Western Renaissance lady wearing a pashmina shawl in the painting has "trafficked for strange webs with

Eastern merchants"; but the commerce between East and the West goes beyond this web (which may be a symbol) into the realm of the spirit; she is a symbol of the eternal soul in its incarnations both Pagan and Christian as Leda and as St. Anne. It is the same thought that runs through Yeats's 'Statues' as the poem moves from Pythagoras in the ancient world to Pearse in modern Ireland. Both Pater and Yeats speak of the relation of the eternal soul to its perfect embodiment in art. Pater's interpretation of 'Mona Lisa' emphasizes the idea of the soul transcending the cycles of life and death in its constant reincarnations:

> She is older than the rocks among which she sits; Like the vampire, she has been dead many times, and learned the secrets of the grave; and has been a diver in deep seas, and keeps their fallen day about her and trafficked for strange webs with Eastern merchants, and as Leda, was the mother of Helen of Troy, and as, Saint Anne, the mother of Mary; and all this has been to her but as the sound of lyres and flutes, and lives only in the delicacy with which it has moulded the changing lineaments, and tinged the eyelids and hands.[8]

No wonder this prose passage of Pater's on 'Mona Lisa' moved Yeats so much that he chose to print it as the first poem in his edition of the *Oxford Book of Modern Verse* which appeared just two years before he composed his poem 'The Statues.'[9]

One archetypal symbol runs through the world's cultures; it is based on the belief of a form perfectly realizing the spirit within as illustrated by Apollo, the Buddha and Hamlet. Pater too expresses a similar thought regarding 'Mona Lisa' as a symbol of this idea:

> The fancy of a perpetual life, sweeping together ten thousand experiences, is an old one; and modern philosophy has conceived the idea of humanity as wrought upon by and summing up in itself, all modes of thought and life. Certainly Lady Lisa might stand as the embodiment of the old fancy, the symbol of the modern idea. . . .[10]

Yeats's 'Statues' employs proper names both historical and fictional making them pregnant with complex and obscure meanings to convey his occult conviction of the spiritual and aesthetic intimations of the great forms of traditional art.

## II

In spite of the constant experiment in poetic idiom, Yeats remains in his style as in his philosophy a traditionalist. Commenting on the allusiveness of style, he says:

> A poetical passage cannot be understood without a rich memory, and like the older school of painting appeals to a tradition, and that not merely when it speaks of 'Lethe warf' or 'Dido on the wild sea banks' but in rhythm, in vocabulary; for the ear must notice slight variations upon old cadences and customary words, all that high breeding of poetical style where there is nothing ostentatious, nothing crude, no breath of parvenu or journalist.[11]

Custom and ceremony are an integral aspect of Yeats's world-view, and style for him is "but high breeding in words and argument."[12]

We have illustrated one aspect of this allusiveness in his use of proper names modified by his own associations of ideas. There is also another important aspect of this allusive technique where words and cadences echoed from great writers of the past are almost conspicuously used in order to enrich his meaning. Critics have often pointed these out.[13] The lines,

> Another Troy must rise and set,
> Another lineage feed the crow,
> Another Argo's painted prow
> Drive to a flashier bauble yet,[14]

though ultimately deriving from Virgil, are an echo in rhythm and words of Shelley's lines,

> A loftier Argo cleaves the main,
> Fraught with a later prize;
> Another Orpheus sings again,
> And loves, and weeps, and dies.[15]

This kind of allusiveness enriches his words and rhythm by reminding the reader of literary tradition. But there is a more significant ambiguity achieved by this allusiveness in some poems. Yeats's poem 'The Man and the Echo' and 'A Bronze Head' illustrate his use of allusion for enriching meaning.

'The Man and the Echo' contains a significant allusion to Hamlet's famous soliloquy, 'To be or not to be, that is the question' in the word "bodkin" in the lines, "There is no release / In a bodkin or disease." Elsewhere Yeats uses the phrase "Hamlet's bodkin."[16] The word is thus a deliberate echo of Shakespeare's play. Its use here lights up the mood of the poem. It is the soliloquy of a man meditating on the events of his life, questioning them, and wondering about his ultimate destiny in death. The *persona* of the poem is thus a Hamlet-like character. Critics[17] who approach the poem biographically tend to identify the speaker of the soliloquy as Yeats. It is of course obvious that these lines have reference to Yeats's own life:

> Did that play of mine send out
> Certain men the English shot?
> Did words of mine put too great strain
> On that woman's reeling brain?

These incidents are common to Yeats and Hamlet. It is therefore likely that the speaker of the solilioquy is a composite one of a Hamlet-like Yeats. The word "question" too is probably a recollection of Shakespeare's *Hamlet*, where its recurrence has been commented upon by critics.[18] "All that I have said or done . . . Turns into a question. . . ." The question with which the poem ends seeking the mystery of life after death, "O Rocky voice, / Shall we in that great night rejoice?" is a Hamlet-like meditation. The line "Body gone he sleeps no more"[19] is probably another allusion to the line "To die: to sleep; No more" in Hamlet's soliloquy, 'To be or not to be, that is the question.' By such significant allusions, especially by the use of key words taken from *Hamlet*, the poem builds up an image of a speaker deliberately ambiguous, half Yeats and half Hamlet. We might say that the mask that Yeats puts on in this poem is that of Hamlet. In *Autobiographies* he speaks of the impression made on his boyish mind by Irving's Hamlet, "For many years Hamlet was an image of heroic self-possession for the poses of childhood and youth to copy, a combatant of the battle within myself" (p. 29). Stallworthy observes that the portraits of his middle years imitate Hamlet in dress and manner.[20] Thus 'The Man and the Echo' is spoken by Yeats wearing the mask of Hamlet. This fits in with the mood of his last poems where he is often turning to the tragic heroes of Shakespeare for his masks: "Myself must I remake / Till I am Timon and Lear." It is the mood of tragic gaiety in them: "Hamlet and Lear are gay."

Thus the key words echoed from *Hamlet* in this poem make it comparable to Laforgue's monologues of Hamlet of which he must have read in Symon's *Symbolist Movement in Literature*.[21] Thus words like "question," "bodkin," "sleep no more," form a cluster illuminating for the discerning reader the whole meaning of the poem as the expression of an ambiguous speaker wearing a mask fusing Yeats and Hamlet. A recognition of the allusiveness of the language and its function enhances the complex suggestiveness and the total meaning of the poem for the discerning reader.

Another poem with the same technique of deliberate ambiguity in the *persona* of the poem is 'A Bronze Head,' (1939). Here also the same cluster of verbal echoes from Shakespeare illuminates the theme. The phrase "*hysterica passio*" is a quotation from *King Lear*. There are other equally significant if less apparent verbal echoes from the play. The word "nothing" in close proximity with this phrase is also another echo from the play. The word is repeated frequently in *King Lear*, and it is first used by Cordelia. From these associations with Cordelia in the first stanza the poem moves by natural transition to the word "gentle" in the phrase "a most gentle woman." It recalls Lear's words about Cordelia, ". . . Her voice was ever soft, / Gentle, and low—an excellent thing in woman" (V. iii. 272–73). The lines, ". . . in a breath / a mouthful held the extreme of life and death" is also probably an echo of Lear's words over the dead Cordelia, "If that her breath will mist or stain the stone, / Why, then she lives." "Propinquity" is not a very common word, and probably derives from Yeats's recollections of Lear's words to Cordelia, "Here I disclaim all my paternal care, / Propinquity and property of blood," (I.i.112–13). The thought and the phrasing in the words of the poem, "I had grown wild / And wandered murmuring everywhere, 'My child, my child!'" recall Lear's words in the recognition scene after his mad wanderings, ". . . I think this lady / To be my child Cordelia," (IV.vii.69–70). "Ancestral pearls" in the poem recalls the phrase in *King Lear* "as pearls from diamonds dropped" (IV.iii.21–22).

This cluster of words echoed from *King Lear* has a bearing on the meaning of the poem. Critics have said that the bronze head is that of Maud Gonne. As usual Yeats is interpreting biographical experience in terms of myth, and the myth here is that of Lear and Cordelia. The speaker of the poem is Yeats wearing the mask of Lear almost exactly as in 'The Man and the Echo' the mask he puts on is that of Hamlet. Cordelia may be described as "Human, superhuman," or "supernatural." There is much in *King Lear* that suggests this by indirection: Lear says to her in the recognition scene, "You are a spirit, I know. When did you die?" (IV.i.49.) Yeats's words could apply to Cordelia. The scene in which these words are spoken are in Lear's imagination somewhere beyond the grave in eternity:

> You do me wrong to take me out of the grave
> Thou art a soul in bliss; but I am bound
> Upon a wheel of fire, that mine own tears
> Do scald like molten lead.
>
> (IV.i.45–58)

The thought in Lear's mind is somewhat that of Christ's Harrowing of Hell or the raising of Lazarus. Probably the phrase "tomb-haunter" is suggested by this association. "This foul world in its decline and fall" is an apt description of the atmosphere of Shakespeare's play, while the line "Heroic reverie mocked by clown and knave" is a typically Yeatsian interpretation of the experience of Lear and Cordelia. Their scorn of all things external is suggested by the lines, "Propinquity had brought / Imagination to that pitch where it casts out / All that is not itself." Yeats's sense of Cordelia's attitude in the face of her anticipated tragedy, and her stern and uncompromising position at the beginning of the play is beautifully interpreted in the lines,

> But even at the starting post, all sleek and new
> I saw the wildness in her and I thought
> A vision of terror that it must live through
> Had shattered her soul.

These verbal echoes from Shakespeare's play help to carry the fusion of fact and myth in the poem, and the reader who brings what Yeats calls a rich memory of literary tradition will discover through it the way to this fusion. The speaker is half Yeats and half

Lear, as the subject of the poem is at once Maud Gonne and Cordelia.

It is this "double vision" in these two poems that gives them their rich concentration of phrase, word and suggestion. At any rate, these allusions point to the influence of Shakespearean tragedy on Yeats's idea of tragic joy and its expression in these poems.[22] The awareness of the verbal echoes from Shakespeare and their significance enrich the meaning of the poems.

This technique of allusiveness in language not only draws from Shakespeare, but also from Yeats's reading of Oriental classics. The refrain "What then?" in the poem 'Plato's Ghost' is an exact verbal and thematic echo of the same refrain, *thathah kim*, in a Sanskrit poem of Bhartrihari's.[23] The motto for *Responsibilities 'How am I fallen from myself, for a long time now / I have not seen the Prince of Chang in my dreams'* is a quotation from Confucius indicating the tenor of social and philosophical thought in Yeats modeled on that of the Chinese philosopher. The poems in *Responsibilities* and several other poems in the succeeding sections deal with the Confucian themes of the way of the superior man in his reverence for tradition, dynastic rule, aristocracy, custom and ceremony. The words "custom" and "ceremony" become loaded in Yeats with special almost esoteric meanings as in the following lines:

> How but in custom and in ceremony
> Are innocence and beauty born?
> Ceremony's a name for the rich horn,
> And custom for the spreading laurel tree.[24]

## III

These four kinds of complexity dealt with in this and the last chapter throw light on Yeats's craft of words at work in shaping a style to convey his own distinctive meanings to the reader by what he calls the process of words taking "light from mutual reflection."[25] These words run through his work like "a trail of fire over precious stones"[26] linking poem to poem, and thus unifying his work into a whole. This is achieved by the use of nouns and epithets which gather special meanings through repetition and association in various contexts, proper names that are used somewhat symbolically in poems like 'The Statues,' literary echoes from classics that enrich the meaning of whole poems like 'The Man and the Echo,' and 'A Bronze Head,' and finally by Yeats's coinage of original and significant compound epithets that carry condensed meanings.

As Yeats himself is aware, he is following the French symbolist philosophy of langauge and poetic idiom in shaping his vocabulary. To spiritualize words, to make them evocative and induce states of trance or meditation—this is one of the aims of the symbolist experiment with words and sounds. Yeats would certainly have sympathized with what Symons writes of Mallarmé's philosophy of poetic language:

> Words, he has realized, are of value only as a notation of the free breath of the spirit; words, therefore must be employed with an extreme care, in their choice and adjustment, in setting them to reflect and chime upon one another; yet least of all for their own sake, for what they can never, except by suggestion, express. . . . The word treated indeed with a kind of "adoration" as he says is so regarded in a magnificent sense, in which it is apprehended as a living thing, itself the vision rather than the reality; at least the philtre of the evocation.[27]

Such words, Symons adds, have a liberating principle, the spirit is extracted from matter; they have an "elaborate and instantaneous magic of language, without the formality of an after all impossible description." What Empson says of literary ambiguity is true of Yeats's poems:

> Indeed, what often happens when a piece of writing is felt to offer hidden riches is that one phrase after another lights up and appears at the heart of it; one part after another catches fire, so that you walk about with the thing for several days.[28]

Some of the best poems of Yeats are written in a kind of peculiarly visionary idiom. Poems like 'Byzantium,' 'Blood and the Moon,' and 'A Bronze Head,' are examples of the use of complex words revealing a characteristically Yeatsian mystique of style as craft.

## CHAPTER V
# THE MAKING OF THE STANZA

THE WORDS "MEASUREMENT" and "form" are key words in Yeats's aesthetic. He writes in 'Under Ben Bulben':

> Measurement began our might:
> Forms a stark Egyptian thought,
> Forms that gentler Phidias wrought.

Throughout his career we find him constantly striving to realize these qualities of "measurement" and "form" in his work. The message he addresses to poets,

> Irish poets, learn your trade,
> Sing whatever is well made,
> Scorn the sort now growing up
> All out of shape from toe to top,[1]

and his protest against "This filthy modern tide" and "its formless spawning fury" are indicative of the importance he attaches to the well-made poem—"sculpture of rhyme"—or statue.[2] Yeats's achievement in the handling of a variety of meters, stanzaic patterns, rhyme schemes and rhythmic modulations is as sensitive as it is immense. It gives him a permanent place among the masters of English prosody. Some of his most famous poems like 'When You Are Old,' 'The Lake Isle of Innisfree,' 'Sailing to Byzantium,' 'Lullaby,' have a rhythmic appeal to the ear that defies analysis. Yeats's drafts reveal his patient and meticulous toil in their making. He quotes William Morris's words on reading poetry, "I have taken great pains to write these poems and I am not going to read them as if it was prose."[3] Yeats emphasizes both in his theory and practice the need to make poetic rhythm a vehicle of the imagination or spiritual experience.

His initial statements reveal the importance he attached to the function of rhythm in poetry. Poetry must become imaginative once again by casting out of it all that is not poetry; the brooding on scientific opinion, the preoccupation with social or political subjects must be given up in order that poetry may recover its lost spirituality: this change in substance must be accompanied by a change in rhythm:

> With this change of substance, this return to imagination, this understanding that the laws of art, which are the hidden laws of the world, can alone bind the imagination, would come a change of style, and we would cast out of serious poetry those energetic rhythms, as of a man running, which are the invention of the will with its eyes always on something to be done or undone; and we would seek out those wavering, meditative, organic rhythms, which are the embodiment of the imagination, that neither desires nor hates, because it has done with time, and only wishes to gaze upon some reality, some beauty; nor would it be any longer possible for anybody to deny the importance of form, in all its kinds, for although you can expound an opinion, or describe a thing, when your words are not quite well chosen, you cannot give a body to something that moves beyond the senses, unless your words are as subtle, as complex, as full of mysterious life, as the body of a flower or of a woman.[4]

This emphasis on an "organic" rhythm with a "mysterious life" of its own and the symbolic correspondence between the "laws of art" and "the laws of the world" is central to Yeats's feeling for poetic form and metrical effectiveness. According to him a poem "gives a body to something that moves beyond the senses." He writes to Katharine Tynan about Henley's poems:

> To me Henley's great fault is his form. It is never accidental but always preconceived. His poems are forced into a mould. I dislike the school to which he belongs. A poem should be a law to itself as plants and beasts are. It may be ever so much finished, but all finish should merely make plain that law. (1888)[5]

He has the same dissatisfaction with Poe's 'Raven': "Its execution is a rhythmical trick. Its rhythm never lives for a moment, never once moves with an emotional life" (1899).[6] Again in another letter to his father, he elaborates the idea of an organic rhythm:

Rhythm implies a living body, a breast to rise and fall, or limbs that dance, while the abstract is incompatible with life . . . I separate the rhythmical and the abstract. They are brothers but one is Abel and one is Cain. In poetry they are not fused for we know that poetry is rhythm but in music hall verses we find an abstract cadence, which is vulgar because it is apart from imitation. This cadence is a mechanism, it never suggests a voice shaken with joy or sorrow as poetical rhythm does. It is but the noise of the machine and not the coming and going of the breath. (1916)[7]

It is this sensation of movement or a natural voice shaken with joy or sorrow that he finds in the lyric poetry of Elizabethan and Jacobean poets. Writing to Grierson he says:

The over childish or over pretty or feminine element in some good Wordsworth and in much poetry up to our date comes from the lack of natural momentum in the syntax. This momentum underlies almost every Elizabethan and Jacobean lyric and is far more important than simplicity of vocabulary . . . Perhaps in our world only an amateur can seek it all – unless he keep to the surface like Kipling – somebody like myself who seeks it with an intense unnatural labour that reduces composition to four or five lines a day. (1926)[8]

Art must conceal art, and Yeats's intense labor in composition is generally hidden under a surface of easy and spontaneous writing. He valued the nonchalance of verse which concealed this intense effort. He writes to Dorothy Wellesley complimenting her on this quality: "Those little poems of yours are nonchalant, and nonchalance is declared by Castiglione essential to all true courtiers so it is to warty lads and poets" (1936).[9] This "nonchalance" which conceals labor is probably implied in the lines in 'Adam's Curse':

. . . A line will take us hours maybe;
Yet if it does not seem a moment's thought,
Our stitching and unstitching has been naught.

In 'Ego Dominus Tuus' he nostalgically laments the loss in modern art or poetry of the "old nonchalance of the hand."

Yeats, like all great poets, is guided in his metrical experiments by his own half-instinctive or intuitive feeling for the correspondences between theme or imagery and verse rather than by an elaborate scientific knowledge of prosody. Robert Bridges who was well-known for his prosodic criticism and theories and whom Yeats knew was probably of some help to him in the theory of versification. He writes to Bridges:

I too would much like to discuss with you questions of rhythm for though I work hard at my rhythm I have but little science on the matter and as a result probably offend them. Without a consistent science it is difficult to distinguish between licence and freedom. (1897)[10]

However, it is from his response to verse when it is spoken well and with passion that he derives the rules of rhythm to guide him. He writes to Patrick Campbell:

Your acting seemed to have the perfect precision and delicacy and simplicity of every art at its best. It made me feel the unity of the arts in a new way. I said to myself this is exactly what I am trying to do in writing, to express myself without waste, without emphasis. To be impassioned and to have a perfect self-possession, to have a precision so absolute that the slightest inflection of voice, the slightest rhythm of sound or emotion plucks the heart-strings. (1901)[11]

It is the union of precision of articulation in dramatic poetry or lyric that fascinates Yeats, and which is for him the beauty of the music of speech. It is to this ideal of the living human voice under the stress of feeling or passion that poetry must return:

Racine and Shakespeare wrote for a little stage where very little could be done with movement, but they were as we know careful to get a great range of expression out of the voice. Our art, like theirs without despising movement, must restore the voice to its importance, for all our playwrights, Synge just as much as myself, get their finest effects out of style, out of the expressiveness of speech itself. (1904)[12]

Yeats also emphasizes the need for incantation in poetry in his search for an expressiveness in language that would approximate to magical effect or trance-inducing states of mind:

I want to do a little play which can be acted and half chanted and so help the return of bigger poetical plays to the stage. This is really a magical revolution, for the magical word is the chanted word. (1899)[13]

Yeats's metrical craftsmanship is a continuous effort to realize in his poems some of these ideals in versification. In this process he experimented in a variety of stanzaic forms, rhyme schemes, and line lengths. From the comparatively swift moving ballads to the slow meditative cadences of his poems of reverie we have a wide range of modulation and rhythmic flow. Apart from the baffling variety of this achievement, the ultimate secret of the magic of rhythm has its roots in the intuitive or subconscious response of writer and reader. This secret is not laid bare by any statistical data of rhymes, or stanzaic patterns, or the minutiae of scansion. However there is an element of deliberate craftsmanship in the making of the structure of verse, and to this extent, it is possible and may be worthwhile to subject poems to metrical analysis. Yeats has a variety of metrical forms, but for the sake of concentration we shall focus attention on his eight-line stanza form. It starts appearing early in his work. He writes some of his most famous poems in the middle period in this stanza form, and it is the form in which some of his famous last poems are written. By tracing the growth and the evolution of this form from the beginning to the end, and analyzing some representative samples we can get some idea of the craftsmanship of Yeats's versification at work on achieving a sensitive correspondence between the mood and the rhythmic movement.

## II

Yeats's early love poetry is often reminiscent of the courtly love poetry of the Elizabethan period in particular of Wyatt's love lyrics. Even the titles of Yeats's poems like 'The Lover Asks Forgiveness Because of His Many Moods,' 'He Tells of a Valley Full of Lovers,' 'He Tells of the Perfect Beauty,' 'The Lover Pleads with His Friend for Old Friends,' 'He Wishes for the Cloths of Heaven' recall the titles of such poems by Wyatt as 'The Lover Complaineth Himself Forsaken,' 'The Lover Hopeth of Better Chance,' 'The Lover Professeth Himself Constant.' There is also considerable similarity between the structure of Yeats's poems and that of Wyatt's. What Southall says of Wyatt's metrical qualities is also true to Yeats:

> English speech rhythms are phrasal and consequently Wyatt's 'English verse' tends to fall into phrasal units separated by pauses, the value of which depend upon the significance of the communication, so that the

fundamental character of the rhythm is due to the requirements of intonation.[14]

Very often Wyatt combines these phrasal units followed by pauses with a run-on movement, or *enjambement*, reinforced by a syntax where the periodical sentence covers a whole stanza. Other features of Wyatt are internal rhymes, repetitions of words, and refrains. Yeats recaptures the mood and tone of the courtly love poets of the Elizabethan age. His aspiration was to love "in the old high way of love," in which lovers thought love should be "So much compounded of high courtesy / That they would sigh and quote with learned looks / Precedents out of beautiful old books." Yeats's love poetry is full of these "precedents out of beautiful old books." The inflections of voice speaking in these poems recall the tone of poets like Wyatt. Some of the features of this poetry like its periodic syntax covering a whole stanza, its internal rhymes, its phrasal structure and its *enjambement* are employed by Yeats.

One of the early examples of this kind of poetry in the eight-line stanza is 'The Pity of Love' (1892). If we ignore the colon at the end of the second line, it is a one sentence poem. The colon at the end of the second line allows a heavy pause before the catalogue of the threatening things is made in the phrases

> The folk who are buying and selling,
> The clouds on their journey above,
> The cold wet winds ever blowing,
> And the shadowy hazel grove
> Where mouse-grey waters are flowing.

These phrases with their diverse images suggestive of the entire world of nature as a perpetual menace emphasized by the verbs in the present continuous tense and the heavy movement caused by the consecutive stresses in the line "the cold wet winds ever blowing" culminate in the last line with its significantly emphatic initially stressed syllable, "Threaten the head that I love."

'He Tells of the Perfect Beauty' (1895), is another poem in the same courtly tradition. Like 'The Pity of Love' it is a single eight-line stanza poem, but in its movement and cadence it is a distinct advance over the earlier poem in so far as it has a slow and deliberately weighted movement. Its phrases are more varied in their contrasted length; the metrical variation and the repetitions of sounds and words give the single sentence of the poem its unified tone and structure. The poem begins with the heavily stressed line with its compounds, "O cloud-pale eyelids, dream dimmed eyes." Its assonance, alliteration, stresses and the medial and terminal pauses make the line heavy and slow. These two phrases with their pauses are now followed by a long continuous movement in the next four lines which contrast the labor of the poets with the "unlabouring brood of the skies." The variation in the inverted trochaic foot after the initial regular iamb in the second line of the poem enriches the meaning:

> The poets labouring all their days
> To build a perfect beauty in rhyme
> Are overthrown by a woman's gaze
> And by the unlabouring brood of the skies.

After this sustained movement with its run-on lines, the poem dies down to a gradual paused cadence in its final lines:

> And therefore my heart will bow, when dew
> Is dropping sleep, until God burn time,
> Before the unlabouring stars and you.

The same perfection of a fine metrical pattern is achieved in another courtly monologue entitled 'A Poet to His Beloved' (1899). This is another single stanza poem with eight lines in one sentence; but the repetitions of phrases like "I bring," "Numberless dreams," "white woman," and of the word "passion" and the repeated back vowels and diphthongs in "white," "worn," "tide," "fire," "time" and "horn" give the poem its unified tone. The phrases are more regularly measured, each phrase consists of two lines; the major pause at the end of the sixth line prepares the way to the closing cadence with its single line phrases:

> I bring you with reverent hands
> The books of my numberless dreams,
> White woman that passion has worn
> As the tide wears the dove-grey sands,
> And with heart more old than the horn
> That is brimmed from the pale fire of time:

> White woman with numberless dreams,
> I bring you my passionate rhyme.

'He Wishes for the Cloths of Heaven' (1899) is the most famous of these single stanza poems, and it gathers the rich fruit of Yeats's early experiments in a slow retarded movement weighted with pause and phonetic repetitions. A series of internal rhymes and echoes runs through the lines:

> Had I the heavens' embroidered cloths,
> Enwrought with golden and silver light,
> The blue and the dim and the dark cloths
> Of night and light and the half-light,
> I would spread the cloths under your feet.

The inverted syntax gives the opening lines a certain momentum although subdued by the pauses. The major pause at the end of the fifth line is necessary for the change of tone in the next three lines, "But I, being poor, have only my dreams; / I have spread my dreams under your feet." The last line begins with a final initial variation: "Tread softly because you tread on my dreams." The extra stressed syllable gives it its slow dying quality. In these single stanza poems we have considered Yeats's experiments with diverse rhyme schemes. 'He Wishes for the Cloths of Heaven' is however a novel experiment in that the same words are used as rhymes: "cloths," "light," "cloths," "light," "feet," "dreams," "feet," and "dreams."

## III

The theme of courtly love traditionally has an allegorical or symbolical level at which human and divine love are mingled. 'The Travail of Passion' (1896) and 'The Lover Speaks to the Hearers of His Songs in Coming Days' (1895) are both eight line single stanza poems which develop the theme of the relation of mortal to immortal love. These have a visionary quality, and the intention of the verse is to induce an experience of reverie in which the human and the transcendental elements are fused. It is significant that while in the poems like 'The Pity of Love,' 'He Tells of the Perfect Beauty' and 'He Wishes for the Cloths of Heaven' the lines are generally octosyllabic, in these visionary poems Yeats uses deliberately a much longer line with at least twelve syllables in them. The alexandrine is traditionally associated with a slow rhythm suited to contemplation, and critics have always noticed the gradualness of the cadence it brings to the Spenserian stanza aptly described by Hazlitt as the "music of our waking dreams." It is this music suitable to reverie that makes Keats choose the stanza for his 'St. Agnes Eve,' and Tennyson for the opening of the 'The Lotus Eaters.' Yeats has a number of poems where the entire stanza consists of alexandrines. Here at least the line (according to Pope) "That like a wounded Snake, drags its slow Length along" is not needless. They answer to a felt need to convey the mood of the poet:

> The purpose of rhythm, it has always seemed to me, is to prolong the moment of contemplation, the moment when we are both asleep and awake, which is the one moment of creation, by hushing us with an alluring monotony.[15]

It is this purpose that is fulfilled in the long lines of 'The Travail of Passion.' The poem is steeped in Biblical imagery describing the passion of Christ, and the speaker Yeats has in mind is probably Mary Magdalene in her love for Christ implied in the images of the "hair," "perfume," and "Lillies of death-pale hope, roses of passionate dream." These images are suggestive of her washing the feet of Christ with perfumes and her hair. For a speaker like this visionary Mary Magdalene, Yeats brings an appropriate rhythm with the appropriate imagery. The lines have twelve-syllables each, and the pauses which are distinct both at the end of the lines and in the middle add to the slow weighted tone of the speech with its note of long suffering love and its reverie: the metrical variations are precise in so far as they call our attention to the most significant epithets with their compression and their phonetic density also adds to the weight of the lines:

> When the flaming lute-thronged angelic door is wide;
> When an immortal passion breathes in mortal clay;
> Our hearts endure the scourge, the plaited thorns, the way
> Crowded with bitter faces, the wounds in palm and side,
> The vinegar-heavy sponge, the flowers by Kedron stream;

The last phrase after the images of suffering prepares the transition from a mood of despair to hope, and it is this mood of hope that is expressed in the changed tone of the concluding lines:

> We will bend down and loosen our hair over you,
> That it may drop faint perfume, and be heavy with dew,
> Lillies of death-pale hope, roses of passionate dream.

Like 'The Travail of Passion,' 'The Lover Speaks to the Hearers of His Songs in Coming Days' is also probably Biblical as its images of a singer who wove songs for his beloved, the myrrh and frankincense suggest Solomon around whom Yeats writes the later poems 'Solomon and Sheba,' and 'Solomon and the Witch.' Once again the long twelve-syllable line is used throughout its eight-line stanza with the same effect of a rhythm that "prolongs the moment of contemplation" by its "alluring monotony." The line "O Women, kneeling by your altar-rails long hence," sets the mood of the poem, while the heavily stressed lines, "And smoke from this dead heart drifts through the violet air / And covers away the smoke of myrrh and frankincense" and the final line with its polysyllabic words "Amid the hovering, piteous, penitential throng" precisely capture in their movement the sense or feeling of an otherworldly atmosphere.

We can group together 'The Travail of Passion,' 'The Lover Speaks to the Hearers of His Songs in Coming Days,' with 'The Valley of the Black Pig' (1896) and 'He Tells of a Valley Full of Lovers' (1897). These four poems form a visionary group dealing with the supernatural world. They are all written in the same twelve-syllabled line with an occasional extra metrical syllable. After his early experiments in a variety of rhymes for the poems in octosyllabic verse, Yeats appears to be finally settling down to a favorite rhyme scheme *abbacddc* in all these four poems. They mark a clear stage in his handling of the eight-line stanza. As a rule he seems to associate the long alexandrine with poems which have a visionary content. A more frequent use of medial and terminal pauses in these lines gives them their retarded movement. Consecutive stresses or significant variations of the basic iambic pattern giving the thought its precisely adapted tune show Yeats's craftsmanship in metrical nuances:

The dews drop slowly and dreams gather:

We who still labour by the cromlech on the shore,
The grey cairn on the hill, when day sinks drowned in dew,
. . .
Master of the still stars and of the flaming door.

And I dreamed my lost love came stealthily out of the wood
With her cloud-pale eyelids falling on dream-dimmed eyes.

'The Magi' (1913) belongs to a later period of Yeats's work. It is the culmination of the early experiments in the long-lined eight-line single stanza poem based upon one periodic sentence. Here again Yeats appears to need a long slow moving line for his prophetic or visionary mood. The lines have a pause at the end, and the repetitions of words and sounds (the diphthong *ai* is the base of thc vowel music of the poem), the consecutive stresses, the general monosyllabic quality exploding into the polysyllabic words at the end of the poem suggestive of the long patient quest of the Magi and the suddenness of the incarnation make it one of the finest examples of Yeats's craftsmanship in metrical and phonetic technique:

Now as at all times I can see in the mind's eye,
In their stiff, painted clothes, the pale unsatisfied ones
Appear and disappear in the blue depth of the sky
With all their ancient faces like rain-beaten stones,
And all their helms of silver hovering side by side,
And all their eyes, still fixed, hoping to find once more,
Being by Calvary's turbulence unsatisfied,
The uncontrollable mystery on the bestial floor.

Though the later Yeats turned more frequently to the ballad stanza for its lightness and its tripping movement, or the *ottava rima* for a more spacious medium, still occasionally he returns to the long lines of these early visionary poems. However, they have now a clearer closeness to common speech rhythm and its colloquial flavor. The contrast between the tone of 'The Magi' (1913) and 'His Phoenix' (1915), written in a more dramatic idiom, is clear. Although the rhyme scheme is the same, the lines in 'His Phoenix' are generally understressed with only four or five stressed syllables while in 'The Magi' each line has at least six stressed syllables:

> There is a queen in China, or maybe it's in Spain,
> And birthdays and holidays such praises can be heard
> Of her unblemished lineaments, a whiteness with no stain,
> That she might be that sprightly girl trodden by a bird;
> And there's a score of duchesses, surpassing womankind,
> Or who have found a painter to make them so for pay
> And smooth out stain and blemish with the elegance of his mind:
> I knew a phoenix in my youth, so let them have their day.

The same myths as in the earlier poems are here—Leda and the Swan, the phoenix, and the beautiful women of legend or romance. But though the long line and the stanza structure are there the tone is far from that of the slow-moving brooding imagination of the poems like 'The Travail of Passion,' or 'The Magi.' The old repetitions, and the spondaic heaviness with their "alluring monotony" have disappeared in a radically changed diction and rhythmic quality. Yeats is deliberately reacting against his own early manner here. Perhaps he could not have continued at this pace or rhythm or even realistic language because his temperament and atmosphere of thought needed a slower movement though the languor of his early rhythm also needed to be vitalized by more dramatic energy and intensity. How to combine the maximum poetic rhythm—those wavering meditative cadences which he preferred to the faster rhythms of didactic or propagandistic verse with the maximum dramatic gesture in language and tone of voice is the main problem of Yeats's later work, and the solution of this problem in the harmony of the two is the most characteristic aspect of his metrical or poetic achievement. The finest poems of this later period achieve this fine harmony without sacrificing poetic rhythm to the excesses of common speech.

Of this harmony the eight-line stanza of the poem 'Upon a Dying Lady' (1913) is a significant example. The play world which is the theme of Yeats's lyrics about tragic joy is the subject of the poem, and the rhythm moves between the long lines of the opening eight-line stanza with its stateliness and pictorial effect, and the lighter playful shorter lines in section iv. The opening stanza recalls the early parallels with their slow movement, their pauses, their spondaic heaviness, and phonetic texture; but these are combined here with a judicious measure of common speech rhythm and common vocabulary; the effect is that of a still picture of the dying lady in all her grace on her death-bed:

> With the old kindness, the old distinguished grace,
> She lies, her lovely piteous head amid dull red hair
> Propped upon pillows, rouge on the pallor of her face.

Every line has a medial pause, while the last line has a fine balance in its construction with the two phrases with their initially stressed syllables, "propped" and "rouge." The alliteration "propped," "piteous," "pillows," "pallor," the repetition of the word "old," and the spondaic effect of "dull red hair" are characteristic. The succeeding lines with fewer stressed elements have a faster tempo and a more conversational tone:

> She would not have us sad because she is lying there,
> And when she meets our gaze her eyes are laughter-lit,
> Her speech a wicked tale that we may vie with her,
> Matching our broken-hearted wit against her wit,
> Thinking of saints and of Petronius Arbiter.

In a tone that mingles Blake's long lines with his shorter lyrics—suggestive of the mingling of experience and innocence—Yeats's poem moves from the long lines of the opening section to the short lines of section iv which recall the lightness of a nursery rhyme in their lilt and rhymes. Life and death are but play:

> She is playing like a child
> And penance is the play,
> Fantastical and wild
> Because the end of day
> Shows her that some one soon
> Will come from the house, and say—
> Though play is but half done—
> 'Come in and leave the play.'

Like the poem 'Upon a Dying Lady,' 'Meditations in Time of Civil War' (1921) consists of varying stanzaic patterns. The last section muses on a pageant of history presenting 'Phantoms of Hatred and the Heart's Fullness and of the Coming Emptiness,' "Frenzies bewilder, reveries perturb the mind; / Monstrous familiar images swim to the mind's eye." Once again, as in 'The Magi' "the mind's eye" supplies the theme of prophecy. As Yeats describes a phase of culture in its fulfillment, the old slow-moving cadence returns with the long line, though the languorousness of the early rhythm is almost eliminated: the rhyme scheme, *ab ab cd cd* is the same:

> Their legs long, delicate and slender, acquamarine their eyes,
> Magical unicorns bear ladies on their backs.
> The ladies close their musing eyes. No prophecies,
> Remembered out of Babylonian almanacs,
> Have closed the ladies' eyes, their minds are but a pool
> Where even longing drowns under its own excess;
> Nothing but stillness can remain when hearts are full
> Of their own sweetness, bodies of their loveliness.

In spite of repetitions of the words and the pauses, the lines have a new flexibility in which the musing imagination and its reverie are combined with a style somewhat less remote if not quite familiar than that of 'The Magi.' The full measure of this harmony in its easy mingling of tone that is at once poetic and conversational, at once active and contemplative, or near and remote, is achieved in the next stanza:

> Nor hate of what's to come, nor pity for what's gone,
> Nothing but grip of claw, and the eye's complacency,
> The innumerable clanging wings that have put out the moon.

The conversational phrases reach a contrapuntal movement and tone of the Tennysonian onomatopoetic line with its nasal quality. The balanced harmony of the conversational tone with the long alexandrine reaches its culmination in the last stanza:

> I turn away and shut the door, and on the stair
> Wonder how many times I could have proved my worth
> In something that all others understand or share;
> But O! ambitious heart, had such a proof drawn forth
> A company of friends, a conscience set at ease,
> It had but made us pine the more. The abstract joy,
> The half-read wisdom of daemonic images,
> Suffice the ageing man as once the growing boy.

These are Yeats's metrical experiments in the eight-line hexameter stanzas over a period of nearly thirty years. Many of these experiments in the earlier part of his work are single stanza poems, although in poems like 'Upon a Dying Lady' and 'Meditations in Time of Civil War' they mingle with other stanzaic patterns in the same poem. Most of them deal with visionary or supernatural themes. Like Blake, who uses the long line for his prophetic books, Yeats also seems to find them suitable for expressing reverie or the fantasies of the dreaming imagination. In many of these poems he has a single sentence with the old Elizabethan periodic structure. The rhyme scheme is generally *ab ba cd dc* or *ab ab cd dc*. While the poems written in this form before 1914 tend to a formal structure and a heavily weighted rhythm, the later poems show the stanzaic pattern absorbing Yeats's changed dramatic tone or idiom.

## IV

The results of these experiments in the poems of courtly love in the early eight-line single stanza verses, and the poems of the longer and the slow moving alexandrines for visionary suggestiveness and contemplation culminate in the mature work of Yeats in which we find a large number of poems in the *ottava rima*.[16] Some of his most famous poems like the Byzantine poems, 'In Memory of Major Robert Gregory,' 'A Prayer for my Daughter,' 'The Gyres,' and 'The Statues' are written in the eight-line stanza of decasyllablic lines though there are variations in rhyme schemes, and occasionally in the length of the lines. In these the typical idiom of the later Yeats—half-dramatic and half-incantatory—mingling colloquial elements with more remote phrasing and vocabulary emerges in its energy and beauty. At the same time the defects of a too familiar tone or of a too remote dreamy voice are avoided. Alike in style and metrical pattern these poems represent the high water-mark of Yeats's craftsmanship in verse.

'In Memory of Major Robert Gregory' (1919) is Yeats's first long poem in the eight-line stanza form with the iambic pentameter as its base. The rhyme scheme is *aa bb cd dc* varying the *ottava rima* scheme of *ab ab ab cc* and Yeats's own early fondness for *ab ba cd dc*. George Saintsbury (*Manual of Prosody*, London, 1920), mentions two principal eight-line stanzas of decasyllables in English—one with a rhyme scheme *ab ab bc bc* and the other (*Ottava rima*) *ab ab ab cc*. Yeats seems to prefer a fourth rhyming word (*d*) in several places making a rhyme scheme of *aa bb cd dc*. The language is apparently conversational and the rhythm is that of common speech as in its opening line, "Now that we're almost settled in our house / I'll name the friends . . ." However Yeats achieves both dignity and music by a careful structuring of his periodic sentence with its flowing involutions, by the juxtaposition of common monosyllabic words with remoter polysyllabic ones, and by a steady acceleration of the pace of the movement of the stanza from its conversational beginnings to its enjambed grandeur, and by carefully studied variations of the basic pattern:

> Lionel Johnson comes the first to mind,
> That loved his learning better than mankind,
> Though courteous to the worst; much failing he
> Brooded upon sanctity
> Till all his Greek and Latin learning seemed
> A long blast upon the horn that brought
> A little nearer to his thought
> A measureless consummation that he dreamed.

The last five lines of the stanza have a progressively increasing momentum because they constitute one single metrical phrase. "Brooded" and "blast" are effective metrical variations. The long back vowels in "A long blast upon the horn that brought" lead on to the suggestion of infinitude in the stately polysyllabic grandeur of the line "A measureless consummation that he dreamed."

The rhetorical momentum of an interrogative sentence accelerated by the run-on movement of the lines and a heightened dramatic tone combined with a conversational slant typical of Yeats's stanzaic patterns are illustrated by the following stanza. After the fifth line, with its climactic questioning tone the stanza shifts to a falling rhythm in its opening inversions and pauses, and settles down to a quiet even tenor:

> What other could so well have counselled us
> In all lovely intricacies of a house
> As he that practised or that understood
> All work in metal or in wood,
> In moulded plaster or in carven stone?

Soldier, scholar, horseman, he,
And all he did done, perfectly
As though he had but that one trade alone.

Yeats uses the line "Soldier, scholar, horseman, he," as a refrain in three consecutive stanzas. As the sixth line it starts a new movement of the verse with its inversions, its four pauses, and the emphasis the normally unstressed "he" obtains because of its placing at the end of the line between two pauses.

'A Prayer for My Daughter' follows in 1919 with the same rhyme scheme as that of 'Major Robert Gregory.' However the stanzaic structure is a new experiment in combining long lines and short lines, the long lines sometimes being alexandrines while the short ones vary from seven syllables to nine. The rhythmic pattern in its movement captures something of the "excited reverie" sought to be communicated by the poem: the number of stresses in a line varies from five to three, and the length of the metrical phrases is equally varied. The same progress of the stanza from a low key in a conversational tone to the more incantatory conclusion we have noticed before in Yeats can be found here:

| stresses | | syllables |
|---|---|---|
| 6 | I have walked and prayed for this young child an hour | (11) |
| 5 | And heard the sea-wind scream upon the tower, | (10) |
| 4 | And under the arches of the bridge, and scream | (11) |
| 4 | In the elms above the flooded stream; | (9) |
| 3 | Imagining in excited reverie | (11) |
| 3 | That the future years had come, | (7) |
| 3 | Dancing to a frenzied drum, | (7) |
| 4 | Out of the murderous innocence of the sea. | (12) |

The effective use of polysyllabic words, the juxtaposition of familiar with remote words, the continuous flow of the rhythm matching the sense, the nasal onamatopoetic sounds, and the subtle effect of the variations in line lengths are illustrated in the lines,

And have no business but dispensing round (11)
Their magnanimities of sound. (8)

The conclusion of the stanza coming to a level tranquil tone can be felt in the variations of the iambic pattern in lines like,

> O may she live like some green laurel
> Rooted in one dear perpetual place.

'Sailing to Byzantium' (1927) is Yeats's finest poem in the eight-line stanza. It replaces the rhyme schemes of 'In Memory of Major Robert Gregory' and 'A Prayer for My Daughter' by the more regular *ottava rima* rhyme scheme of *abababcc*. The somewhat experimental devices of combining short lines and long lines now give place to the more traditional pattern of uniformly decasyllabic lines. Within this conventional frame of the pattern, Yeats achieves a remarkably individual style or voice. If, as Middleton Murry says, style is the combination of the maximum of impersonality with the maximum of personality, 'Sailing to Byzantium' is a fine example. The quality of freshness within the pattern is achieved by the suppleness or flexibility of the rhythm, the precision of the variations of the pattern, the measure of the metrical phrase harmonizing with the mood or image, the significant use of polysyllabic Latinized words, and the shading off of the colloquial idiom into the incantatory liturgy.

The opening sentence owes its dramatic emphasis to its brevity and its stressed elements: "That is no country for old men." From the spondaic variations in "old men" the transition to the antithetical phrase "the young" is both natural and effective. The succeeding lines with their pauses, and dense compounds reflect in their structure, imagery and phonetic quality something of the dense sensuality of all nature: man, bird and beast are all subject to the same sensual decay: the polysyllabic word "generations" in "dying generations" (reminiscent of Keats's "hungry generations" in 'The Ode to a Nightingale') is a fine phonetic prelude to the perpetual death of all created things huddled together in the lines with their consonant clusters emphasized by their metrical position and alliteration, "The salmon-falls, the mackerel-crowded seas, / Fish, flesh, or fowl. . . ." The Oriental sense of the soul enmeshed in the world of sensual illusion is expressed by the emphatic position of the word "Caught" in the beginning of the line "Caught in that sensual music all neglect" while the world of the soul's infinity is suggested by the polysyllabic "Monuments" again with the initial stress in the line "Monuments of unageing intellect." From this line to the opening line of the second stanza there is both a semantic and phonetic contrast with the words "unageing" and "aged" emphasizing it: "An aged man is but a paltry thing." The metrical phrasing of the succeeding lines, their tendency to run-on movement, the variations emphasizing tragic joy in the midst of physical decay, and the return to the polysyllabic conclusion contribute to the perfect adjustment of metrical and phonetic effect to the meaning:

> A tattered coat upon a stick, unless
> Soul clap its hands and sing, and louder sing
> For every tatter in its mortal dress,
> Nor is there singing school but studying
> Monuments of its own magnificence.

The last lines of the stanza with their monosyllabic regularity and even tenor are suggestive of the soul which in the Oriental phrase of *The Upanishads* "have gone over to the other shore" from this bank and shoal of time. The pilgrim's progress at an end now, the voice in the third stanza is one of religious surrender and prayer, and the lines with their slow movement suggest a liturgical tone: once again the stanza picks up the word "holy" from the last line of the preceding stanza, and the metaphor of music that runs through the poem is recalled in the phrase "singing masters of my soul." The descent of these sages is finely suggested by the falling trochaic inversions in the third line:

> O sages standing in God's holy fire
> As in the gold mosaic of a wall,
> Come from the holy fire, perne in a gyre
> And be the singing-masters of my soul.

The metrical phrases are precise and appropriately varied in their length. The shortest sentence in the poem is "Consume my heart away"; its brevity lends contrast to the next phrase which is longer with its sense of the burden of sick life, and it opens with the stressed word "sick":

> Sick with desire
> And fastened to a dying animal
> It knows not what it is.

The lightly stressed last line with its polysyllabic words is appropriate to the image of a light-winged singing bird symbolizing the redeemed soul: "and gather me / Into the artifice of eternity." The suggestion implicit in the rhythmic nuance of the line is elaborated in the next stanza of the soul redeemed from the body of nature: the flight from time to eternity emerges in the emphasis of the opening lines of the fourth stanza with the stressed initial word, "Once out of nature I shall never take / My bodily form from any natural thing." The next phrase consists of three continuous lines with their run-on movement expressive of the lyrical joy of release from time or nature into some golden permanence. The lines recall Donne's phrase "like gold to airy thinness beat":

> But such a form as Grecian goldsmiths make
> Of hammered gold and gold enamelling
> To keep a drowsy Emperor awake.

In the last three lines the stanza and the poem settles down to a gradually halted slow-paced rhythm in the regular iambic pentameter lines:

> Or set upon a golden bough to sing
> To lords and ladies of Byzantium
> Of what is past, or passing, or to come.

'Sailing to Byzantium' and 'Byzantium' (1930) have often been read as companion poems from the point of view of their themes and symbols. The two also make an interesting contrast in their rhythmic structure. The voice of the *persona* in 'Sailing to Byzantium' is that of an ascetic renouncing the world of nature in quest of eternity. His moods of Buddhistic disgust with sensuality, of prayer and surrender, and of yearning for pure timeless being are beautifully articulated in its tone and its inflections throughout the poem. On the whole we might say that the poem has a level tenor avoiding any sharp rises and falls of the voice. A *retardando* style of music gives its intuitive central stillness of being an appropriately controlled voice. But the voice of the *persona* in 'Byzantium' is one of excited reverie and revelation. As F.A.C. Wilson[17] points out the *persona* of the poem is probably a supernatural spirit revealing to the listener the dynamism of the making of spirits. The rhythm for this communication needs a rapidity of movement to suit the apocalyptic vision, and the poem thus employs an *accelerando* style. Though the stanzas are eight-line, Yeats mingles long and short lines, the shortest being one of four syllables in "All that man is," while the short lines are generally of six syllables. The rhyme scheme is not that of the *ottava rima* as in 'Sailing to Byzantium,' but changes to an arrangement Yeats has used elsewhere—*aa bb cddc*.

The opening lines setting the midnight scene for the revelation and describing the "unpurged images of day" receding have a deliberately paused movement:

> The unpurged images of day recede;
> The Emperor's drunken soldiery are abed;
> Night resonance recedes, night-walkers' song
> After great cathedral gong;

From such a heavily paused beginning the poem moves on to a swifter excited movement as it seeks images or symbols for some fugitive or fleeting vision of the supernatural world; a breathless rhythm for a quick succession of images is appropriate to this changed vision or miracle. The repetitions of sounds, words, the run-on lines, the short phrases, and the metrical inversions give the verse its accelerated pace of lyric swiftness; the wheels as it were from the very motion catch fire to suggest a pageant of swiftly moving flames or flame-like spirits.

> At midnight on the Emperor's pavement flit
> Flames that no faggot feeds, nor steel has lit,
> Nor storm disturbs, flames begotten of flame,
> Where blood-begotten spirits come
> And all complexities of fury leave,
> Dying into a dance,
> An agony of trance,
> An agony of flame that cannot singe a sleeve.

In the previous chapter we noticed the way Yeats uses words with characteristic complexity of meaning in this passage. To this semiprivate vocabulary he now adds rhythmic patterns with which he has been experimenting for a long time. The single periodic sentence covering a whole stanza, the phrasal structure with its pauses contrasted with the run-on lines, the metrical inversions, the short lines contrasted with the long alexandrine last line—all old familiar devices he has tried elsewhere—are brought together to suggest the intensity of the experience. If the words reveal their meanings only to the trained Yeats reader who has followed their usage elsewhere, the rhythmic qualities too require an ear trained to perceive the craftsmanship of the poet culminating in such lines after decades of experiment.

The last stanza both in its dynamic words of action and images like "smithies" and "break," its consonant clusters, its contrast of short and long vowels, and in the final half-Tennysonian onomatopoetic line with its characteristically Yeatsian compounds carries the breathless or apocalyptic voice of the *persona* to its climax:

> Astraddle on the dolphin's mire and blood,
> Spirit after spirit! The smithies break the flood,
> The golden smithies of the Emperor!
> Marbles of the dancing floor
> Break bitter furies of complexity,
> Those images that yet
> Fresh images beget,
> That dolphin-born, that gong-tormented sea.

The Byzantium poems represent the high water-mark of Yeats's metrical craftsmanship even as they represent the complexity of meanings in his diction and symbols. He continues to employ the eight-line stanza for some of his famous last poems like 'The Gyres,' 'The Municipal Gallery Revisited,' 'The Statues,' and 'The Circus Animal's Desertion.' Metrically these poems have no very striking innovations or improvement on the Byzantium poems. In the last poems generally speaking Yeats's language attains a bare naked quality, and he is more concerned with the direct and straightforward projection of his ideas rather than with the communication of states of reverie or trance in evocative words and rhythms. The syntax is altered, it is less involved, and the sentences are shorter; the old periodic sentence with its seventeenth century elaboration tends to disappear. The nonchalance of the run-on movement, the slow drugged cadences with their weighted pauses and phrasal structure, and the general phonetic body of the poems with the old assonance, consonant clusters and word or phrase repetitions now give place to a direct kind of speech which while it gains in dramatic quality loses in incantatory or musical effectiveness. Yeats apparently is less interested in style than in thought and its communication. A deliberate or harsh realistic tone is sometimes his characteristic in the last poems:

> What matter though numb nightmare ride on top,
> And blood and mire the sensitive body stain?

or

> I sought a theme and sought for it in vain,
> I sought it daily for six weeks or so.

or

> . . . Now my ladder is gone,
> I must lie down where all the ladders start,
> In the foul rag-and-bone shop of the heart.

From the more incantatory magic of earlier poems to this bareness denuded of all metrical or rhythmic nuance is a great change. The last poems undoubtedly feature condensed thought and a great deal of obscurity. But their appeal to the ear is not in any sense comparable to that of the earlier poems.

The evolution of Yeats's eight-line stanza form from its early appearance in his work to the end illustrates clearly the subtleties of his metrical craftsmanship. It is a stanzaic form for which he has a clear fondness. It suits the purposes of the various *personae* of his poems. The courtly lover of the Renaissance, the voice of a Mary Magdalene in her love for Christ, the religious visionary looking for another incarnation, the elegiac poet lamenting the death of Major Robert Gregory, the pilgrim sailing to Byzantium, the spirit voice in 'Byzantium'—all these are the masks that Yeats wears in his poems. And all these find in the eight-line stanza the modulations of voice and tone they need for their moods. Thus a wide range of rhythmic effect is achieved in it. In the octosyllabic eight-line stanza it can have the rapidity of 'The Song of Wandering Aengus':

> Though I am old with wandering
> Through hollow lands and hilly lands,
> I will find out where she has gone,
> And kiss her lips and take her hands;
> And walk among long dappled grass,
> And pluck till time and times are done
> The silver apples of the moon,
> The golden apples of the sun.

It reaches a slow cadence in the decasyllabic lines of 'The Everlasting Voices' matching the mood of the poem:

> Have you not heard that our hearts are old,
> That you call in birds, in wind on the hill,
> In shaken boughs, in tide on the shore?
> O sweet everlasting Voices, be still.

It sometimes attains the dramatic energy of a long interrogatory sentence:

> O what if gardens where the peacock strays
> With delicate feet upon old terraces,
> Or else all Juno from an urn displays
> Before the indifferent garden deities;
> O what if levelled lawns and gravelled ways
> Where slippered Contemplation finds his ease
> And Childhood a delight for every sense,
> But take our greatness with our violence?

In a more dreamy or visionary mood, the stanza uses the longer alexandrines as more suited to the visionary theme:

> We who still labour by the cromlech on the shore,
> The grey cairn on the hill, when day sinks drowned in dew,
> Being weary of the world's empires, bow down to you,
> Master of the still stars and of the flaming door.

Are such rhythmic structures the result of deliberate metrical skill or are they the result of instinctive feeling for the music of language and for the precise expression of thought? Yeats himself disowns any serious knowledge of prosody:

> You will notice how bothered I am when I get to prosody—because it is the most certain of my instincts, it is the subject of which I am most ignorant. I do not even know if I should write the mark of accent or stress thus / or thus ˎ .[18]

Though in the last analysis every poet is guided by an unconscious or intuitive sense of the music of his poems or themes, still metrical craftsmanship, involving the arrangement of stresses, the division of phrases and lines, and the making of rhyme schemes is largely a deliberate or conscious activity. Yeats's eight-line stanzas in their diversity of rhythm illustrate a meticulous care or skill in the adjustment of the tune to the theme. Is he guided by a syllabic count of the number of syllables in a line? Or does he make his lines by reckoning the number of feet in them? Or is it a sense for phrasal melody that determines his rhythms? The answer to these questions is not easy. Like all his predecessors he probably uses all these methods as it suits him subject to the overriding sensitivity of ear to the modulations of the human voice and imaginative feeling. Whatever metrical principles may have guided him, there is no doubt that he spends an enormous amount of labor to achieve the fine metrical effects of his verse.

## CHAPTER VI

# THE ART OF THE DRAMATIC POEM

UNDERNEATH ALL THE CHANGES in metrical form and style in Yeats's poetry there is one broad unifying quality of dramatic tone in his work from the beginning to the end. It is significant that 'The Song of the Happy Shepherd'—the first poem in Yeats's *Collected Poems*—should strike a note of a dramatic monologue ending with the exhortation to the listener: ". . . dream thou! / For fair are poppies on the brow: / Dream, dream, for this is also sooth." If this is the dramatic tone in this early lyrical poem, his last poem 'Under Ben Bulben' is also a dramatic monologue in which the *persona* conjures his auditors by oath. The tone is more imperative:

> Swear by what the sages spoke
> Round the Mareotic Lake
> That the Witch of Atlas knew,
> Spoke and set the cocks a-crow.

The fact that the first and the last poem in Yeats are both dramatic monologues is no mere accident. Between the two there is a large number of poems which in varying degrees employ the same tone of a speaker addressing his listeners, and the rhetorical and dramatic gestures that we associate with the monologue. As several critics[1] have observed, the entire direction of Yeats's work is towards this increasingly dramatic form and atmosphere. Very often it expresses itself directly in the monologue; equally frequent is the poem in which conversation dominates; and more striking than either of these is the poem in which two voices confront each other in direct dialectical Platonic dialogue, a kind of poetry which has a special appeal to Yeats. All three spring from the dramatic imagination. Some of Yeats's finest poems owe their vitality to this intense desire to be dramatic. In various degrees his poems suggest to us a *persona* involved in some kind of action, his presence, movement, gesture or voice. Several of his most famous poems open on a dramatic note:

> When you are old and grey and full of sleep,
> And nodding by the fire, take down this book,[2]

or

> Young man, lift up your russet brow,
> And lift your tender eyelids, maid,[3]

or

> Fasten your hair with a golden pin,
> And bind up every wandering tress[4]

or

> There is grey in your hair.[5]

or

> That is no country for old men.[6]

or

> What shall I do with this absurdity—[7]

This habitually dramatic slant is the expression of an imagination that has a strong histrionic cast. Like many of his contemporaries in the late nineteenth century, Yeats tended towards self-dramatization. In manner, dress, and in attitude to life he also expressed this histrionic sense.[8] His theory of masks is to some extent the product of this basic instinctive need for acting. In his wider philosophical speculation he tended to make conflict and dramatic action the essence of history and cosmic cycles. All the world is a stage.[9] Apart from this wider context of general philosophy and native histrionic talent, Yeats's theory of poetry emphasizes the need for the dramatic element in a poem.

One of his axioms in critical theory is the relation between truth and drama: "I was soon to vex my father by defining truth as 'the dramatically appropriate utterance of the highest man.'"[10] He recalls the influence of his father's readings on him:

> At breakfast he read passages from the poets, and always from the play or poem at its most passionate moment. He never read me a passage because of its speculative interest, and indeed did not care at all for poetry where there was generalization or abstraction however impassioned. . . . He did not care even for a fine lyric passage unless he felt some actual man behind its elaboration of beauty, and he was always looking for the lineaments of some desirable, familiar life. . . . All must be an idealisation of speech and at some moment of passionate action or somnambulistic reverie.[11]

Elsewhere Yeats tells how his father would hear of "nothing but drama; personal utterance was only egotism." The roots of poetry are in drama: "All poetry should have a local habitation when at all possible,"[12] and "To me the dramatic is far the pleasantest poetic form."[13] Sometimes a certain Irish delight in the energy and spontaneous joy of excited conversation and dialogue possesses him:

> Let us learn construction from the masters, and dialogue from ourselves. A relation of mine has just written me a letter, in which he says; 'It is natural to an Irishman to write plays; he has an inborn love of dialogue and sound about him, of a dialogue as lively, gallant, and passionate as in the times of great Eliza. In these days an Englishman's dialogue is that of an amateur—that is to say, it is never spontaneous. I mean in real life. Compare it with an Irishman's reckless abandonment and naturalness, or compare it with the only fragment that has come down to us of Shakespeare's own conversation. Petty commerce and puritanism have brought to the front the wrong type of Englishman; the lively, joyous, yet tenacious man has transferred himself to Ireland . . .'[14]

Energy, said Blake, is eternal delight, and the world of drama for Yeats is this world of energy:

> What attracts me to drama is that it is, in the most obvious way, what all the arts are upon a last analysis. A farce and a tragedy are alike in this, that they are a moment of intense life. An action is taken out of all other actions: it is reduced to its simplest forms, or at any rate to as simple a form as it can be brought to without our losing the sense of its place in the

world. The characters that are involved in it are freed from everything that is not a part of that action; and whether it is, as in the less important kinds of drama, a mere bodily activity, a hairbreadth escape or the like, or as it is in the more important kinds, an activity of the souls of the characters, it is an energy, an eddy of life purified from everything but itself. The dramatist must picture life in action, with an unpreoccupied mind, as the musician pictures it in sound and the sculptor in form.[15]

Passion, energy, action and truth are all associated in Yeats's theory of poetry with drama, and therefore a poem in so far as it is passionate must partake of the nature of drama. All art is dedicated to the expression of passion in its purity, its intensity and conflict:

. . . the subject of all art is passion, and a passion can only be contemplated when separated by itself, purified of all but itself, and aroused into a perfect intensity by opposition with some other passion. . . .[16]

Against the background of such ideas, it is easy to see why Yeats tends to regard the poet as a kind of actor wearing some traditionally known mask:

I was about to learn that if a man is to write lyric poetry he must be shaped by nature and art to some one out of half a dozen traditional poses, and be lover or saint, sage or sensualist, or mere mocker of all life; and that none but that stroke of luckless luck can open before him the accumulated expression of the world. And this thought before it could be knowledge was an instinct.[17]

It is out of this instinctive need for traditional masks or poses that Yeats develops his idea of a theatrical, consciously dramatic role for the poet. In his view this is a necessary discipline for him:

There is a relation between discipline and the theatrical sense. If we cannot imagine ourselves as different from what we are and assume that second self, we cannot impose a discipline upon ourselves, though we may accept one from others. Active virtue as distinguished from the passive acceptance of a current code is therefore theatrical, consciously dramatic, the wearing of a mask. It is the condition of arduous full life. One constantly notices in very active natures a tendency to pose, or if the pose has become a second self a preoccupation with the effect they are producing. One notices this in Plutarch's *Lives*, and every now and then in some modern who has tried to live by classical ideas, in Oscar Wilde, for instance, and less obviously in men like Walt Whitman.[18]

Style for Yeats is the speech of this deliberately theatrical person. It is the utterance of a passionate man, and its secret lies in the vitality of the speaker. Dramatic effectiveness is the test of all style:

> I do not mean by style words with an air of literature about them, what is ordinarily called eloquent writing. The speeches of Falstaff are as perfect in their style as the soliloquies of Hamlet. One must be able to make a king of Faery or an old countryman or a modern lover speak that language which is his and nobody else's, and speak it with so much of emotional subtlety that the hearer may find it hard to know whether it is the thought or the word that has moved him, or whether these could be separated at all.[19]

## II

The mask that Yeats puts on in most of the early dramatic monologues is that of the courtly lover. They start appearing in *The Rose* section, and there are nearly a dozen of these in *The Wind Among the Reeds*. These are very different from the usual type of dramatic monologues[20] like Browning's 'Last Duchess' or 'Andrea Del Sarto' or Eliot's 'Prufrock.' Browning's main interest is psychological, and the dramatic monologue is a form he employs for revealing the characters of his men and women at some critical moment. Their setting, idiom, and general atmosphere are realistic, and they are generally in blank verse. The early monologues of Yeats, however, are very different. They are expressions of moods or passions purified of all external circumstance. Thus there is little information given to the reader regarding the setting or locale of the speaker. The speaker and the listener are both highly spiritualized so that no physical or concrete details of appearance or gesture are mentioned. The theme is exalted or romantic love of souls, and this reduces the sense of action or interaction between the speaker and the listener to the very minimum. The language appropriate to such speakers has necessarily to be remote, and the rhythm too such as to suggest this far-away atmosphere. Over all these is spread the quality of imaginative reverie in which the temporal experience becomes the shadow of some transcendental world. In such monologues it is not right to expect the tone of the Duke in Browning's 'Last Duchess' nor that of 'Andrea Del Sarto' or 'Prufrock.' It is apparent that Yeats's early monologues belong to another genre.

'When You Are Old' is representative of the Yeatsian early monologue in which a courtly lover addresses his beloved. The poem opens on a low earthly key in its details of familiar life in these lines, "When you are old and grey and full of sleep, / And nodding by the fire, take down this book." From this familiar setting it looks before and after. The note of contemplation of time and eternity is struck in the next lines augmented by the phonetic and metrical qualities, "And slowly read, and dream of the soft look / Your eyes had once, and of their shadows deep." The second stanza amplifies the retrospect in its recollections of past experience in time. The earthly and spiritual loves are mentioned, and the word 'loved' repeated in each line stresses its use. The first two lines have a comparatively rapid pace: "How many loved your moments of glad grace, / And loved your beauty with love false or true." As memory turns to the spiritual lover, the lines become slower because of the metrical variations: "But one man loved the pilgrim soul in you, / And loved the sorrows of your changing face." The phrase "pilgrim soul" immediately introduces into the poem a level of experience beyond that of time, and suggests future possibilities in eternity. The last stanza begins with a recollection of the setting in the line "And bending down beside the glowing bars," while the concluding lines move from earth to heaven. The word "Love" is capitalized, the mountains overhead, and the lover's face hidden in the stars suggest the eternal world. It is remarkable that the poem beginning with the familiar fireside detail in its setting should end on the word "stars" reminiscent of the same word at the end of Dante's cantos in *Divina Comedia*. The movement is suggestive of a pilgrimage from time to eternity.

> And bending down beside the glowing bars,
> Murmur, a little sadly, how Love fled
> And paced upon the mountains overhead
> And hid his face amid a crowd of stars.

The same theme of the eternity of love and of the soul runs through the other monologues in *The Rose* section like 'The White

Birds,' and 'Who Goes with Fergus?' The speaker in all these poems is the same visionary lover using the tone and idiom suitable to his reveries. 'When You Are Old' is a decasyllabic poem, and its pauses and repetitions give it a slow-cadenced pace. 'The White Birds' is more distinctly visionary, and it appropriately employs a sixteen syllable line for its more distant horizon:

> I am haunted by numberless islands, and many a Danaan shore,
> Where Time would surely forget us, and Sorrow come near us no
> more;
> Soon far from the rose and the lily and fret of the flames would we be,
> Were we only white birds, my beloved, bouyed out on the foam of the
> sea!

'Who Goes with Fergus?' is somewhat more dramatic since the opening sentence is an interrogative one—a device frequently used by Yeats either at the beginning or end of the poem to give it the tone of a man speaking. Unlike 'The White Birds' the lines are shorter being octosyllabic, and they also move faster:

> Who will go drive with Fergus now,
> And pierce the deep wood's woven shade,
> And dance upon the level shore?

The speaker then turns to a pair of lovers whom he addresses:

> Young man, lift up your russet brow,
> And lift your tender eyelids, maid,
> And brood on hopes and fear no more.

*The Wind Among the Reeds* contains the largest number of these monologues. These are: 'The Lover Tells of the Rose in His Heart,' 'The Fish,' 'He Mourns for the Change That Has Come Upon Him and His Beloved, and Longs for the End of the World,' 'He Bids His Beloved Be at Peace,' 'He Remembers Forgotten Beauty,' 'A Poet to His Beloved,' 'He Gives His Beloved Certain Rhymes,' 'The Lover Asks Forgiveness Because of His Many Moods,' 'He Tells of the Perfect Beauty,' 'He Thinks of Those Who Have Spoken Evil of His Beloved,' 'The Lover Pleads with His Friend for Old Friends,' 'The Lover Speaks to the Hearers of His Songs in Coming Days,' 'He Wishes His Beloved Were Dead,' and 'He Wishes for the

Cloths of Heaven.' It is clear even from the titles themselves that these are monologues supposed to be spoken by an imaginary lover to his beloved.

These poems generally revolve round the theme of Platonic and spiritual love like the poems in *The Rose* section. They are dramatic only in the sense that they have a *persona* and one or two listeners. Other extrinsic aspects of the dramatic monologue like stage setting, gesture, interaction between the speaker and the listener, and a familiar idiom and tone are almost deliberately kept out. The monologues in *The Rose* poems mentioned only the eyes or eyelids of the beloved. The only change in concrete detail is the added reference in these poems to the hair of the beloved.[21] Hair, pearl-pale hands and eyes are all that the lover mentions in his addresses. These women are phantoms of the spiritual world, and their hair, eyes and hands are often used as complex words with symbolic meanings. A woman goes out to meet her lover in the world hereafter; only her hair and eyes are mentioned:

> The shadowy blossom of my hair
> Will hide us from the bitter storm.
>
> O hiding hair and dewy eyes,
> I am no more with life and death,
> My heart upon his warm heart lies,
> My breath is mixed into his breath.[22]

The same supernatural association with hair is even more clearly expressed in another poem, 'He Wishes His Beloved Were Dead.' Somewhat reminiscent of Browning's 'Porphyria's Lover,' the speaker would possess his beloved for ever in eternity:

> Nor would you rise and hasten away,
> Though you have the will of the wild birds,
> But know your hair was bound and wound
> About the stars and moon and sun.

With these associations, phrases like "dim hair,"[23] "Fasten your hair with a golden pin,/ And bind up every wandering tress,"[24] "bind up your long hair and sigh;/ And all men's hearts must burn and beat,"[25] "Crumple the rose in your hair,"[26] "And cover the pale blossoms of your breast/ With your dim heavy hair,"[27] "Half close your eyelids, loosen your hair,"[28] "We will bend down and loosen our hair over you,"[29] are all vaguely suggestive of the stylized spiritual or half angelic women of Pre-Raphaelite art. The monologues are linked together by one or two significant personal details which have a symbolic quality relating the mortal world to the immortal. It is because of this twilight world, and its dim and dreamy air that the physical attributes of the persons or other concrete particulars are deliberately reduced or eliminated. Occasionally a recognizable familiar voice somewhat close to common speech may be heard as in 'The Fish':

> Although you hide in the ebb and flow
> Of the pale tide when the moon has set,
> The people of coming days will know
> About the casting out of my net,
> And how you have leaped times out of mind
> Over the little silver cords,
> And think that you were hard and unkind,
> And blame you with many bitter words.

But generally the idiom and the rhythm are far removed from that of common speech, and tend to harmonize with the atmosphere of reverie in many of these monologues.

Thus both in *The Rose* section and *The Wind Among The Reeds* the mask that dominates the monologues is that of the courtly or mystic lover addressing a woman who is half supernatural and half earthly. Yeats's intention seems to be to express the shadowy twilight world of spiritual love, or make the poems convey a pure flame-like passion. In approaching these dramatic monologues it is necessary to keep in mind this intention. Otherwise we might apply to them criteria derived from Browning or Eliot such as realistic setting, characterization, psychological insight and common speech—criteria that are not appropriate to the judgement of these monologues. It is true that the absence of these qualities makes them somewhat undramatic. But Yeats's purpose is very different, and his technique or craftsmanship in them deliberately avoids the features of Browning or Eliot.

However in the later monologues of Yeats written after 1900 there is a distinct change in his technique of handling the form. The change is brought about by his love poetry taking a more concrete or earthly turn shedding some of its early dreamy or Petrarchan airiness. The lover emerges as a real human being, and the beloved assumes a more earthly form, and the address has a more familiar ring. The change is also brought about by a new satirical vein which expresses itself in some of the monologues like 'Paudeen.' It coincides with the period when Yeats is busy writing and producing his plays. Thus lessons of his experience as a dramatist are now applied to the making of poems with the result that these become more dramatic in style and atmosphere. From the section entitled *In The Seven Woods* to the *Last Poems* the monologues become increasingly realistic in *persona*, language, setting, and situations. We shall briefly consider some of these monologues representative of this later period i.e., after the composition of the monologues in *The Rose* (1893) and *The Wind Among the Reeds* (1899).

The poems *In The Seven Woods* illustrate the change towards more actuality in the lover and his beloved. We can feel this change in the lines,

> I thought of your beauty, and this arrow,
> Made out of a wild thought, is in my marrow.
> There's no man may look upon her, no man,
> As when newly grown to be a woman,
> Tall and noble but with face and bosom
> Delicate in colour as apple blossom.[30]

Or in the lines,

> O never give the heart outright,
> For they, for all smooth lips can say,
> Have given their hearts up to the play.[31]

Or in these,

> But O, in a minute she changed—
> O do not love too long,
> Or you will grow out of fashion
> Like an old song.[32]

It is a new consciousness of the reality of human experience in time, and a corresponding turning away from the infinite that makes the situations and setting also more real:

> And I that have not your faith, how shall I know
> That in the blinding light beyond the grave
> We'll find so good a thing as that we have lost?
> The hourly kindness, and the day's common speech,
> The habitual content of each with each
> When neither soul nor body has been crossed. (1910)[33]

With this sense of the value of human experience there comes into these monologues a style and a setting entirely different from those of the early poems. 'Reconciliation' unites a colloquial idiom with its involved syntax appropriate to a real situation or mood, and one can sense in it some quality of Browning's love lyrics. The moment of the poem allows contrasts of the past and the present; the opening lines look back on what had happened:

> Some may have blamed you that you took away
> The verses that could move them on the day
> When, the ears being deafened, the sight of the eyes blind
> With lightning, you went from me, and I could find
> Nothing to make a song about but kings,
> Helmets, and swords, and half-forgotten things
> That were like memories of you.

After the pause the conversation turns from the past to the present:

> —but now
> We'll out, for the world lives as long ago;
> And while we're in our laughing, weeping fit,
> Hurl helmets, crowns, and swords into the pit.

The poem ends on a vivid bodily gesture, "But, dear, cling close to me; since you were gone, / My barren thoughts have chilled me to the bone."

'A Drinking Song' (1910) is a complete contrast in mood, tone, and gesture to the courtly manner of the earlier monologues:

> Wine comes in at the mouth
> And love comes in at the eye;
> That's all we shall know for truth
> Before we grow old and die.
> I lift the glass to my mouth,
> I look at you, and I sigh.

'Broken Dreams' (1919) has a striking dramatic opening in the lines,

> There is grey in your hair.
> Young men no longer suddenly catch their breath
> When you are passing.

Once again this poem deals with the theme of temporal and spiritual love, and asserts the certainty that "in the grave all, all, shall be renewed." But this transcendental note notwithstanding the atmosphere of the poem is familiar as in the phrases, "By merely walking in a room," "All day in the one chair." In contrast to the highly spiritual detail of eyes and hair in the early monologues, this poem emphasizes the bodily appearance of the beloved, and cherishes its very human imperfection. A certain Chaucerian distinctness of feature and vivid human form emerges in the stanza giving the speaker and the listener a genuine earthly touch:

> You are more beautiful than any one,
> And yet your body had a flaw:
> Your small hands were not beautiful,
> And I am afraid that you will run
> And paddle to the wrist
> In that mysterious, always brimming lake
> Where those that have obeyed the holy law
> Paddle and are perfect. Leave unchanged
> The hands that I have kissed,
> For old sake's sake.

The later poems of Yeats in *Words for Music Perhaps* (1933), *A Full Moon in March* (1935) and *Last Poems* (1939) include among them some of the most realistic detail with a romantic flavor. Of the realistic variety 'Crazy Jane and the Bishop' is a typical example. The priest with "an old book in his fist" is pictured in disgusting detail by Crazy Jane:

The Bishop has a skin, God knows,
Wrinkled like the foot of a goose,
(*All find safety in the tomb.*)
Nor can he hide in holy black
The heron's hunch upon his back,
But a birch-tree stood my Jack:
*The solid man and the coxcomb.*

For all this apparent realism, the poem indirectly expresses Yeats's habitual belief in an after-life in the refrain "*All find safety in the tomb.*"

'Those Dancing Days Are Gone' expresses in the form of a lyrical monologue blending realistic detail and tragic joy an aspect of Yeats's final philosophy of life and death:

Come, let me sing into your ear;
Those dancing days are gone,
All that silk and satin gear;
Crouch upon a stone,
Wrapping that foul body up
In as foul a rag:
*I carry the sun in a golden cup,*
*The moon in a silver bag.*

'Ribh at the Tomb of Baile and Aillinn' is one of the finest of Yeats's dramatic monologues. Its blank verse gives it a more flexible speech rhythm. The setting is indicated, and the speaker's voice is one of familiarity: "Because you have found me in the pitch-dark night / With open book you ask me what I do." The old periodic sentence pattern now yields to shorter and more direct forms:

Mark and digest my tale, carry it afar
To those that never saw this tonsured head
Nor heard this voice that ninety years have cracked.

The actuality of the setting and the speaker are both a foil and a transition to the supernatural quality of the theme which is again the theme of love beyond the grave:

Here in the pitch-dark atmosphere above
The trembling of the apple and the yew,
Here on the anniversary of their death,

> The anniversary of their first embrace,
> These lovers, purified by tragedy,
> Hurry into each other's arms; these eyes,
> By water, herb and solitary prayer
> Made acquiline, are open to that light.

The poem comes back in a circular manner to the point at which it begins recalling after this supernatural note its familiar setting:

> Though somewhat broken by the leaves, that light
> Lies in a circle on the grass; therein
> I turn the pages of my holy book.

'To Dorothy Wellesley' is another monologue where the familiar and the strange enrich each other by their close juxtaposition. The "moonless midnight of the trees," "famous old upholsteries," "the horizon's bought strange dogs," "Great Dane that cannot bay the moon / And now lies sunk in sleep," "The Proud Furies each with her torch on high" are images which in their tension or opposition of realistic detail and weird supernaturalism make up the stuff of which the characteristic Yeatsian last poems are made.

Of this technique, which brings together the familiar and the remote in imagery, setting and speech, Yeats's last poem 'Under Ben Bulben' is a fine example. The *persona* of the poem is a supernatural being like the *persona* of 'Byzantium'; the setting with its allusions to Shelley's *Witch of Atlas* is supernatural; the auditors who belong to the human world are conjured in the name of the immortals. The voice is commanding, awesome, and spectral; the repetition of the word "Swear"—an echo of the ghost's voice in *Hamlet*—twice in initially stressed positions sets the key of the whole poem:

> Swear by what the sages spoke
> Round the Mareotic Lake
> That the Witch of Atlas knew,
> Spoke and set the cocks a-crow.
>
> Swear by those horsemen, by those women
> Complexion and form prove superhuman,
> That pale, long-visaged company
> That air in immortality
> Completeness of their passions won;

Now they ride the wintry dawn
Where Ben Bulben sets the scene.

The form and style of the dramatic monologue in Yeats change with his evolution over a period of nearly forty years. From the early heavily romantic atmosphere, imagery and reverie in the courtly monologues like 'When You Are Old' or 'A Poet to His Beloved' he moves into poems where there is more concrete detail in setting, in the appearance of the *persona* involved, and also in language as in 'Broken Dreams.' A maturer dramatic style, and a vision of life where the natural and the supernatural mingle grow together. His finest dramatic monologues are those where familiar images of everyday life and myths and symbols of his transcendental vision are woven together in a manner that suggests the effect of Shakespeare's technique mingling romance and realism in *A Midsummer Night's Dream* and *The Tempest.*

## III

The dramatic monologue of the courtly lover in Yeats recalls Elizabethan parallels in sentiment and style. It represents an aspect of his dramatic imagination. The conversation poems of which he had a few represent another aspect of the same imagination, and recall some of the most famous conversation poems like those of Coleridge. These are not so numerous as the dramatic monologues, but they constitute a significant portion of his work in quality if not in quantity. These are 'Ephemera' (1889), 'Adam's Curse' (1904), 'The People' (1919), 'Solomon and the Witch' (1921). Of these the two most representative conversation pieces are 'Adam's Curse,' and 'The People.' They illustrate Yeats's craftsmanship in the making of this kind of poem.

The style of 'Adam's Curse,' is that of common speech in its short, conversational, and informal sentences. The construction of the opening lines in spite of the subdued rhymes reads like that of actual speech:

We sat together at one summer's end,
That beautiful mild woman, your close friend,
And you and I, and talked of poetry.

The phrasal structure with its frequent pauses, and the chatty manner of the line "That beautiful mild woman, your close friend" immediately suggest the spontaneity of the speaker's voice and style. Unlike the periodic syntax of some of his dramatic monologues and lyrics, the syntax here continues to remain more or less at this level, short, crisp, colloquial and informal:

> I said: 'A line will take us hours maybe;
> Yet if it does not seem a moment's thought,
> Our stitching and unstitching has been naught.'

The colloquial word "maybe," and the image of stitching and unstitching give the poem an everyday level of talk and experience. Other images that follow continue this everyday quality:

> Better go down upon your marrow-bones
> And scrub a kitchen pavement, or break stones
> Like an old pauper, in all kinds of weather;
> . . .
> Of bankers, schoolmasters, and clergymen
> The martyrs call the world.'

A mingling of narration and reported speech, however, allows scope for slight differences of tone and language. After this colloquial utterance, the narrator moves to a slightly more eloquent manner in the run-on lines that follow:

> And thereupon
> That beautiful mild woman for whose sake
> There's many a one shall find out all heartache
> On finding that her voice is sweet and low
> Replied:

Again the direct speech brings the tone down from this elevation to a lower key with its parenthesis—an essential feature of conversational style:

> 'To be born woman is to know—
> Although they do not talk of it at school—
> That we must labour to be beautiful.'

From this commonplace level of thought the poem rises to its climax in the exalted meditation of the third stanza. Lovers of the old world, love compounded of "high courtesy," "learned looks," "Precedents out of beautiful old books" give the lines their romantic and distant loftiness of tone, and make them all the more striking as they emerge from a background of commonplace talk. The stanza begins and ends on a familiar note but in between there is an elaborate moment of finely wrought musical rhythm:

> I said: 'It's certain there is no fine thing
> Since Adam's fall but needs much labouring.

After this short and direct sentence we have the lofty quality of these lines with their continuous rhythm, and Latinized style:

> There have been lovers who thought love should be
> So much compounded of high courtesy
> That they would sigh and quote with learned looks
> Precedents out of beautiful old books.

After this elevated moment we come down to the commonplace conclusion in the line, "'Yet now it seems an idle trade enough.'"

The poem then moves to its final quietude of setting amplifying the "summer's end" of the first line. A hush descends on the talkers after the exalted moment of the third stanza—a fine silence rich with meditation on what has been said. The mood and the setting harmonize beautifully:

> We sat grown quiet at the name of love;
> We saw the last embers of daylight die,
> And in the trembling blue-green of the sky
> A moon, worn as if it had been a shell
> Washed by time's waters as they rose and fell
> About the stars and broke in days and years.

The worn moon, the dying daylight, and the silence make an appropriate prelude to the lines describing the exhausted and silent lovers who look before and after and pine for what is not. The lines have a dying cadence:

> I had a thought for no one's but your ears:
> That you were beautiful, and that I strove

To love you in the old high way of love;
That it had all seemed happy, and yet we'd grown
As weary-hearted as the hollow moon.

Thus in its rise, progress and conclusion, 'Adam's Curse' represents the pattern of a beautiful conversation poem. In its style it has the naturalness and spontaneity necessary for its art. A chance occurrence, a ruminating mood, and then a flight of exalted meditation are according to Max Schulz the characteristics of the conversation poems of Coleridge.

The conversation poem traces two calm-exaltation-calm parabolas. In each poem Coleridge starts conversationally in the hushed air of a momentarily silenced earth. Moved by a sudden thought or incident, his mood rises to a climax or exalted philosophical or ethical meditation and then sinks from this impassioned tone through quiet talk to the silence that had reigned in the beginning.[34]

Yeats's 'Adam's Curse' closely conforms to this pattern of a conversation poem that evolves from modest beginnings to a moment of deep feeling and thought, and then sinks into a large, significant silence into which the conversation dies in a paradoxical fulfillment of eloquent suggestion.

'Adam's Curse' is a fine example of a rhymed conversational poem. Strong rhymes when they are prominent can make the conversation poem somewhat artificial, and deprive it of naturalness. Pope's 'Epistle to Arbuthnot' is mainly conversational, but the rhymes give point to the heroic couplet, and to the epigrammatic phrasing. Pope deftly combines the couplet with the spontaneity of natural talk. The rhymes in 'Adam's Curse' are largely weak, and they are so subdued that the conversational naturalness is not diminished. Rhymes like "poetry" and "maybe", "weather" and "together," "school" and "beautiful," "be" and "courtesy," "thing" and "labouring" are not very distinctly heard. Others like "enough" and "love," "strove" and "love," and "grown" and "moon" are at best half-rhymes. Such rhymes indicate Yeats's intention not to let them dominate the poem.

After this experiment in indistinct rhymes, it is only natural he should try blank verse in another conversation poem entitled 'The People.' The poem begins with a dramatic gesture in the question:

> 'What have I learned for all that work,' I said,
> 'For all that I have done at my own charge?

The lines, "I might have lived, / And you know well how great the longing has been," with the parenthesis add another conversational turn to the opening lines. After this beginning in a low key, the poem moves to a more excited moment in a long run-on verse paragraph of continuous rhythm where the idiom harmonizes with the nostalgia for the old romantic world of Castiglione's *Courtier*:

> Where every day my footfall should have lit
> In the green shadow of Ferrara wall;
> Or climbed among the images of the past—
> The unperturbed and courtly images—
> Evening and morning, the steep street of Urbino
> To where the Duchess and her people talked
> The stately midnight through until they stood
> In their great window looking at the dawn;
> I might have had no friend that could not mix
> Courtesy and passion into one like those
> That saw the wicks grow yellow in the dawn.

After this rising lofty note the poem descends into the everyday world of strife and heat in the lines of the lady's reply and the contrasted realism of the phrases "'the drunkards, pilferers of public funds / All the dishonest crowd I had driven away.'" After this exchange between the interlocutors, the poem settles to the hushed conclusion with its thoughtful silence in the lines,

> And yet, because my heart leaped at her words,
> I was abashed, and now they come to mind
> After nine years, I sink my head abashed.

'Adam's Curse' and 'The People' are two of Yeats's most effective conversation poems. Both begin in a casual manner, move to a climax of explanation, and then descend to the silence of meditation. In both the style is that of the natural and spontaneous speaker with the free, somewhat rambling, informal tone of actual speech. Both exemplify a kind of subtle art in creating their apparent artlessness.

## IV

Yeats has a number of poems which can be called dialogue poems. The dramatic monologue implies a speaker or *persona* and one or more hearers. The conversation poem is an interchange in which two or three interlocutors participate. The dialogue poem is one in which we have two persons exchanging arguments in the manner of a dialogue in Plato or an imaginary conversation of Landor. The conversation poem is a mixture of direct and reported speech, and the nature of the interlocutors is to be inferred from their speeches. It is a form particularly suitable for argument and for dialectics. In the conversation poem there is an informal friendly atmosphere. In the dialogue the structure is more logical, coherent, and artificial. In the middle and later poetry of Yeats, the form is frequently used for this purpose. His theory of opposites like the self and the anti-self, and his sense of the conflict between the body and the soul lead him to the composition of such poems where the opposed points of view can be clearly brought out. They are the expression of an inner war within the consciousness of the poet.

Almost from the beginning Yeats has a partiality for these dialogue poems. 'Anashuya and Vijaya' (1889), 'Fergus and the Druid' (1893), and 'The Players Ask for a Blessing on the Psalteries and on Themselves' (1904) are early examples. These are dramatic fragments in which no dialectical debate is involved. 'Shepherd and Goatherd' (1919) is an elegy on the death of Major Robert Gregory, written in a pastoral convention recalling the poetry of Spenser. 'Ego Dominus Tuus,' 'The Phases of the Moon' and 'The Saint and the Hunchback' (all probably written about the same time and published in 1919) revolve round the dialectical themes of individual and cosmic evolution through conflict. 'Michael Robartes and the Dancer' and 'An Image from a Past Life' and 'Solomon and the Witch' appear in 1921, and they too deal with the themes of conflict of various kinds. 'A Dialogue of Self and Soul' and 'The Seven Sages' are published in 1933. The former is an essentially dialectical poem considering the relative claims of the soul and the body. Thus Yeats's experiments with this form cover a period of thirty years.

Not all the poems are successful, but 'Ego Dominus Tuus' and 'A Dialogue of Self and Soul' are justly famous for their thought and structure. 'Ego Dominus Tuus' is a debate between the primary and antithetical selves, the former thought of as masculine and the latter as feminine. The esoteric atmosphere of the poem is created by the symbols in the setting described in the opening:

> On the grey sand beside the shallow stream
> Under your old wind-beaten tower, where still
> A lamp burns on beside the open book
> That Michael Robartes left, you walk in the moon,
> And, though you have passed the best of life, still trace,
> Enthralled by the unconquerable delusion,
> Magical shapes.

We have only to read these lines aloud and compare them with the lines with which 'Adam's Curse' or 'The People' begins to realize the difference in tone. This blank verse structure with its verse paragraph effect built around a periodic sentence gives the poem a loftiness or remoteness in contrast to the intimacy or familiarity of the conversation poem. This setting in which a Faust-like magician is at work at his occult symbols is recalled again towards the end of the poem:

> Why should you leave the lamp
> Burning alone beside an open book,
> And trace these characters upon the sands?

The sense of secrecy and mystery essential to the whole dialogue is again communicated in the lines,

> I call to the mysterious one who yet
> Shall walk the wet sands by the edge of the stream
> And look most like me, being indeed my double,
> And prove of all imaginable things
> The most unlike, being my anti-self,
> And, standing by these characters, disclose
> All that I seek; and whisper it as though
> He were afraid the birds, who cry aloud
> Their momentary cries before it is dawn,
> Would carry it away to blasphemous men.

These repeated references to the magical quality of the search and its nocturnal scene are essential to the total effect of the poem.

They also serve to endow the speaker with a strange supernatural air.

The frequent interrogative sentences, and expressions like "And yet," "Yet surely," "No, not sing," give the poem a conversational or debating tone. In the midst of these colloquial bits, we have stately blank verse when the argument of the poem reaches its climax as in the interpretation of Dante or Keats. A fine blend of direct statement in short sentences with the more involved periodic sentence gives this paragraph a rising crescendo of music appropriate to the theme:

> And did he find himself
> Or was the hunger that had made it hollow
> A hunger for the apple on the bough
> Most out of reach? and is that spectral image
> The man that Lapo and that Guido knew?

After these rhetorical questions we have the answer in a long metrical phrase covering the next four lines:

> I think he fashioned from his opposite
> An image that might have been a stony face
> Staring upon a Bedouin's horse-hair roof
> From doored and windowed cliff, or half upturned
> Among the coarse grass and the camel-dung.

These run-on lines of the periodic sentences are followed for contrast by a short one-line sentence; "He set his chisel to the hardest stone." The climax of the passage is reached in its vivid description of the artist creating his art out of tragic war within himself—the theme of the poem:

> Being mocked by Guido for his lecherous life,
> Derided and deriding, driven out
> To climb that stair and eat that bitter bread,
> He found the unpersuadable justice, he found
> The most exalted lady loved by a man.

'Ego Dominus Tuus' is based on a favorite idea of Yeats about the self and the anti-self while 'A Dialogue of Self and Soul' has a more universal theme of the human conflict between the empirical self and the soul, between the world of sensuous experience and its beauty and the abstract spiritual world of Platonism or Vedanta on the other. If the poem has greater human interest, it is also a more artistically structured poem than 'Ego Dominus Tuus.' It is written in 1933, and by this time Yeats has mastered the intricacies of the eight-line stanza and used it for a number of his masterpieces. He brings to the stanzas of this poem an expert skill. The dramatic quality of the idiom is apparent if we compare the changing voices in the first two stanzas. The voice of the Soul is commanding and awesome. The steep ascent is intensely visualized as the progress from the crumbling battlement through the starlit air and the pole star to the nirvana of ultimate being where there is neither light nor darkness. The quick succession of the images in this ascent, and the imperious voice of the Soul are vividly rendered in the lines:

> My Soul. I summon to the winding ancient stair;
> Set all your mind upon the steep ascent,
> Upon the broken, crumbling battlement,
> Upon the breathless starlit air,
> Upon the star that marks the hidden pole;
> Fix every wandering thought upon
> That quarter where all thought is done:
> Who can distinguish darkness from the soul?

In conception, imagery, and rhythm this is a fine rendering of the effort of the yogi described in *The Upanishads* in his quest for salvation from the cycle of birth and death. The words "summon" and the repetitions of the word "Upon" in successive lines indicative of the leap of the Soul from one plane to another, the stressed syllables in the initial positions, "Set" and "Fix," and the final question give the stanza the cumulative effect of an extraordinary emphasis. The voice of the earth-bound Self with its sensuous yearnings, and its hesitations to accept the world of the Soul in preference to its worldly life is beautifully contrasted in idiom, and rhythm with that of the Soul. The focus on an image of antiquity and beauty in Sato's sword is striking against the background of the imageless world of the Soul in its dark infinite. While the voice of the Soul summons on relentlessly, the voice of the Self lingers in its longing for some earthly experience of the beautiful in touch, color and antique romance. The dynamic rhythm of the first stanza suitable to its steep ascent now yields place to a slow, paused movement of the verse suggestive of some timeless image in time in its stasis:

> My Self. The consecrated blade upon my knees
> Is Sato's ancient blade, still as it was,
> Still razor-keen, still like a looking-glass
> Unspotted by the centuries;
> That flowering, silken, old embroidery, torn
> From some court-lady's dress and round
> The wooden scabbard bound and wound,
> Can, tattered, still protect, faded adorn.

Whatever the philosophical merits of the voice of the Soul, the voice of the Self is more humanistic and therefore more persuasive. In the second section it is this voice that prevails, and there is little doubt that the poet identifies himself, and expects the reader to identify himself, with this voice. In both the dialogue poems we have examined the argument ends with one side winning the debate—the side that the poet sympathizes with.

From the purely poetic point of view, these dialogue poems are somewhat more abstract and didactic than the dramatic monologues and the conversation poems. The dramatic monologue is content with the expression in generally lyrical language of some mood or passion. It thus appeals to experience. It has also a certain impersonal objectivity. The conversation poems with their contemplative or reminiscent or autobiographical quality have a general atmosphere of friendship, intimacy and thoughtfulness, and leave the reader on a note of silent meditation. No case is argued, and no conclusion reached. The dialogue poem is a conscious attempt to present a case, and arrive at a conclusion. Very often the case is an intellectual or metaphysical one, and to this extent the poem is a movement away from rather than towards experience. Hence their comparative lack of human interest. If negative capability is the criterion of good poetry, then the dramatic monologues and the conversation poems stand on a higher level than the dialogue poems.

However in all the three forms we can see the fundamental dramatic bent of Yeats's imagination expressing itself. In the earlier monologues the mask of the courtly lover or the mystic visionary dreaming on things to come helps him to the composition of some beautiful poems. The poetry of Yeats often celebrates his friendships. The conversation poems have thus a fine autobiographical quality since they enshrine precious moments of talk with a peculiarly friendly grace and nostalgic voice. As his imagination becomes obsessed by the theories of conflict both inner and outer, the somewhat Platonic dialogue form appeals to him. To all these forms Yeats brings an appropriate style, setting and atmosphere. They illustrate his meticulous and minute care in adjusting formal pattern to content.

# CONCLUSION

STUDIES IN A POET'S CRAFTSMANSHIP are of value because they enable us to follow the creative process from its dim origins in the first intentions of the poet to its culmination in the end-product of the poem. Stallworthy in his examination of the manuscript revisions of Yeats's poems,[1] and Bradford in *Yeats at Work* have focused attention on the extraordinary labor bestowed by Yeats on the revision of his work. Some knowledge of the labor helps us to enter into the meaning or experience of the poems more fully as it helps us to watch the poet's workshop.

Poets vary in the degree of conscious effort or labor in the making of their poems. They also vary in the importance they attach to this labor. Literary criticism that tends to consider the Romantic poet as the vehicle of inspired spontaneity and the Classical poet as the conscious and disciplined worker oversimplifies the complexity of poetic creation in which both inspiration and toil generally mingle, though in diverse proportions. Yeats describes himself as the last of the Romantics. He often speaks of poetic frenzy or inspiration. For these are for him the essential means of contact with the supernatural in the reality of which he has an intense religious faith. The poet for him is a spiritual medium, or a prophet. At the same time he constantly dwells on the element of labor or toil involved in the making of a poem. He speaks of the "unnatural labour" in writing four or five lines a day. Thus his inspiration imposes its own law of toil on him. The making of a poem implies a dedicated craftsmanship like that of the religious medieval artisan or the Byzantine metal-worker. It is the "secret discipline / Wherein the gazing heart doubles her might." An analysis of his ideas of the nature of this labor and its bearing on poetic vision helps us to realize the importance Yeats attaches to it. No other poet so often alludes to the pain and sanctity of this toil.

This labor at work on the shaping of his vocabulary is an essential characteristic of Yeats. From poem to poem in each section, and from section to section Yeats's complex words gather increasing meaning through repetition, association with other words, in compound epithets and through allusiveness of technique. These complex words by their recurrence give a certain unity to his entire work. By such means Yeats builds up his own special world of words carrying meanings or experience projected into them by his own imagination. Every poet who has some fresh experience or thought to communicate has to extend the range of the meanings of words to meet his own original needs. An examination of Yeats's recurrent epithets, common and proper nouns, and compound phrases reveals the devices employed by him for deepening their connotation. He deepens the experience of a poem for the careful or cultivated reader by an apparently casual but an arresting and significant use of key words from the world's literary tradition of the West and the East.

The art of communication in poetry depends not only on words but on the order of the words. This order is the poet's metrical or rhythmic technique. If original poets reshape the words of a language for their own specific purposes, they also modify their inheritance of metrical patterns to suit their own sensibility. Yeats builds up his own world of poetic rhythm by using stanzaic patterns to express his states of mind or feeling or reverie. Though he disclaims any deep scientific knowledge of prosody, his instinctive ear for the qualities of incantation, cadence and dramatic speech guides him to the achievement of some of his finest rhythms in the language. As a dramatist he is deeply interested in the effect of spoken verse as a performing art, and his poetry is a rewarding experience to all those who enjoy reading it aloud. At a time when conventional patterns give way to free verse generally, Yeats remains deeply traditional in his sense of metrical form. At the same time he achieves the effect of an original voice in the modulations of his verse.

A poet's craftsmanship lies not only in the shaping of his vocabulary and in the order of his rhythmical patterns, but in the building of the structure of a poem as an organic entity. The last chapter examines Yeats at work on the shaping of a form that answers to his needs, his temperament and world-view—the form of the dramatic poem. A lover addressing his beloved in the manner of courtly love, reminiscences of conversations with friends, and poetic or philosophical dialectics are the themes that often make him turn to the dramatic poem. Here too he modifies the traditional dramatic monologue and the conversational poem to suit his own needs. His dramatic imagination finds the dialogue poem an appropriate means for expressing life's conflicts or for carrying on a dialectical debate in verse. In the mingling of familiar language with more elevated idiom, in the inflections of voice and tone, in gesture and in setting Yeats achieves some of his characteristic effects.

It is evident from these considerations that Yeats's work represents a fine synthesis of poetic vision and laborious craftsmanship. In diction it fuses traditional poetic idiom with contemporary speech. In rhythm conventional patterns become alive with a new life in them. In form the Romantic lyric is vitalized by a new dramatic imagination. Behind the apparent ease or naturalness of his poems there lies an enormous amount of labor. A study of this labor bestowed on words, metrical form, and the dramatic structure of some of his significant poems gives the reader some knowledge of the creative process of one of the greatest poets of our time.

# NOTES

## Chapter 1

1. 'In Memory of Major Robert Gregory.' Citations from Yeats in my text are to *The Collected Poems* (Macmillan, Toronto, 1969).
2. 'After Long Silence.'
3. 'Ego Dominus Tuus.'
4. 'Nineteen Hundred and Nineteen.'
5. 'To Dorothy Wellesley.'
6. 'Meditations in Time of Civil War.'
7. Ibid.
8. Ibid.
9. 'Coole Park and Ballylee.'
10. Ibid.
11. 'Sailing to Byzantium.'
12. 'A Dialogue of Self and Soul.'
13. 'Wisdom.'
14. 'The Tower.'
15. 'Under Ben Bulben.'
16. W.B. Yeats, *A Vision* (Macmillan, New York, 1969), p. 279. Cited hereafter as *A Vision*.
17. Cf. 'The Tower' where Plato and Plotinus are considered abstract.
18. W.B. Yeats, *Autobiographies* (New York, 1965), p. 166. Cited hereafter as *Autobiographies*.
19. *A Vision*, p. 280. Yeats returns to this thought of art improving on Gospel books in his poem entitled 'Wisdom.'
20. 'Sailing to Byzantium.'
21. 'Byzantium.'
22. *Autobiographies*, p. 101.
23. Ibid., p. 102.
24. Ibid., p. 102.
25. 'Meditations in Time of Civil War.'
26. Frederick William Roe, ed. *Victorian Prose* (New York, 1947), p. 533. Cited hereafter as *Victorian Prose*.
27. 'Meditations in Time of Civil War.'

28. W.B. Yeats, *Essays and Introductions* (Macmillan, New York, 1961), p. 389. Cited hereafter as *Essays and Introductions.*
29. *Essays and Introductions*, p. 390.
30. Ibid., p. 393.
31. Ibid., p. 394.
32. W.B. Yeats, *Mythologies* (Macmillan, New York, 1959), p. 269. Cited hereafter as *Mythologies*.
33. In *Aratra Pentelici*, Lecture 1, 'The Division of the Arts,' Ruskin does not admit a classification of art into "greater" or "lesser." "No arbitrary line can be drawn between making statues and making toys, between designing cathedrals and designing plows, between painting in oils or water colors, and coloring Christmas cards or lamp shades, between writing plays and writing limericks. 'A blacksmith may put soul into the making of a horseshoe, and an architect may put none in the building of a church. Only exactly in proportion as the soul is thrown into it, the art becomes Fine. . . . Art is the operation of the hand and the intelligence together." *Victorian Prose*, p. 318. Again, in another passage, the same thought occurs: "In general, the three great, or fine, Arts of Painting, Sculpture, and Architecture are thought of as distinct from the lower and the more mechanical formative arts, such as carpentry or pottery. But we cannot, either verbally, or with any practical advantage, admit such classification. How are we to distinguish painting on canvas from painting on china?—or painting on china from painting in glass?—or painting on glass from infusion of color into any vitreous substance, such as enamel?—or the infusion of color into glass and enamel from the infusion of color into wool or silk, and weaving of pictures in tapestry, or patterns in dress? You will find that although, in ultimately accurate use of the word, painting must be held to mean only the laying of a pigment on a surface with a soft instrument; yet, in broad comparison of the functions of Art, we must conceive of one and the same great artistic faculty, as governing *every mode of disposing colors, in a permanent relation on, or in, a solid substance*; whether it be tinting canvas, or dyeing stuffs; inlaying metals with fused flint, or coating walls with colored stone." *Victorian Prose*, p. 355.
34. *Essays and Introductions*, p. 197.
35. Ibid., p. 52.
36. W.B. Yeats, *Uncollected Prose*, ed. John P. Frayne (Columbia Univ. Press, New York, 1970), p. 394. Cited hereafter as *Uncollected Prose*.
37. Cf. Plato, *Ion*: "For the poet is a light and winged and holy thing, and there is no invention in him until he has been inspired and is out of his sense, and the mind is no longer in him: when he has not attained to this state, he is powerless and unable to utter his oracles . . . they do not speak . . . by any rules of art: they are simply inspired to utter that to which the Muse impels them, and that only; . . . for not by art does the poet sing, but by power divine." *Criticism: The Major Texts*, ed. Walter Jackson Bate (New York, 1952), p. 43. Cf. Shelley, *Defense of Poetry*: "Poetry is indeed something divine. . . .Poetry is not like reasoning, a power to be exerted according to the determination of the will. A man cannot say "I will compose poetry." The greatest poet even cannot say it; for the mind in creation is as a fading coal, which as some invisible influence, like an inconstant wind, awakens to transitory brightness; this power arises from within, like the colour of a flower which fades and changes as it is developed, and the conscious portions of our natures . . . when composition begins, inspiration is already on the decline, and the most glorious poetry that has ever been com-

municated to the world is probably a feeble shadow of the original conceptions of the poet. I appeal to the greatest poets of the present day whether it is not an error to assert that the finest passages of poetry are produced by labour and study." *Literary Criticism: Pope to Croce*, ed. G.W. Allen and H.H. Clark (Wayne State Univ. Press, 1962), Vol. 2, pp. 311–312.

38. Cf. T.S. Eliot's dedication of 'The Waste Land' to Ezra Pound calling him "il miglior fabbro" (the better craftsman).
39. *Uncollected Prose*, p. 274.
40. *Autobiographies*, p. 167.
41. 'Crazy Jane Reproved.'
42. *Autobiographies*, p. 364.
43. William Morris, 'Hopes and Fears for Art,' *Victorian Prose*, p. 519.
44. Cf. *A Vision*, pp. 207–208.

"I must now explain a detail of the symbolism which has come into my poetry . . . These two conjunctions (Jupiter and Saturn) which express so many things are certainly, upon occasion the outward-looking mind, love and its lure, contrasted with introspective knowledge of the mind's self-begotten unity, an intellectual excitement. They stand, so to speak like heraldic supporters guarding the mystery of the fifteenth phase. In certain lines written years ago in the first excitement of discovery I compared one to the Sphinx and one to the Buddha." Yeats is referring to his poem 'The Double Vision of Michael Robartes,' where the image of the dancer, an image of art between the Sphinx and the Buddha symbolizes the fifteenth phase, where all thought becomes an image.

O little did she care who danced between
And little she by whom her dance was seen
So she had outdanced thought,
Body, perfection brought.

45. 'Among School Children.'
46. 'All Things Can Tempt Me.'
47. 'In Memory of Major Robert Gregory.'
48. Matthew Arnold, *Preface to Poems*, 1853, *Victorian Prose*, p. 419.
49. *Uncollected Prose*, p. 284.
50. Ibid., p. 288.
51. Ibid., p. 104.
52. Ibid., pp. 285–287.
53. Ibid., p. 423.
54. *Autobiographies*, p. 77.
55. *Essays and Introductions*, p. 87.
56. Ibid., p. 116.
57. Ibid., p. 49.
58. Ibid., p. 225.
59. Ibid., p. 225.
60. Ibid., p. 226.
61. Ibid., p. 228.
62. See H.R. Bachchan, *W.B. Yeats and Occultism* and A. Davenport, 'W.B. Yeats and *The Upanishads*,' *The Review of English studies*, January, 1952, for a discussion of the influence of Yeats's Upanishadic knowledge, gained from Swami Purohit Swami on the 'Supernatural Songs,' 'The Herne's Egg' and *A Vision*.
63. Cf. Richard Ellman, *Yeats: The Man and The Masks* (New York, 1948), pp. 56–69.

64. Cf. *A Vision*, p. 219. Remarking on Paul Valery's poem 'Cimetiere Marin,' Yeats says that he cannot put this poem among his sacred books for in a passage of great eloquence the author rejoices that human life must pass. "I was about to put this poem among my sacred books, but I cannot now, for I do not believe him. My imagination goes some years backward, and I remember a beautiful young girl singing at the edge of the sea. She thought herself alone, stood barefooted between sea and sand; sang with lifted head of the civilizations that there had come and gone, ending every verse with the cry: 'O Lord, let something remain.'"
65. 'The Phases of the Moon.'
66. Cf. *Autobiographies*, p. 242.
67. 'A Prayer for my Daughter.'
68. 'The Statues.'
    It is likely that Yeats borrowed the idea from Oswald Spengler who writes about the relation between Pythagoras' theory of numbers and Greek statues: "When, about 540 B.C., the circle of the Pythogoreans arrived at the idea that *number is the essence of all things*, it was not "a step in the development of mathematics" that was made, but a wholly new mathematic that was born. . . . The most valuable thing in the Classical mathematic is its proposition that number is the essence of all things *perceptible to the senses*. Defining number as a measure, it contains the whole-world feeling of a soul passionately devoted to the "here" and "now." Measurement in this sense means the measurement of something near and corporeal. Consider the content of the Classical art-work, say the free-standing statue of a naked man; here every essential and important element of Being, its whole rhythm, is exhaustively rendered by surfaces, dimensions and the sensuous relations of the parts. The Pythogorean notion of the harmony of numbers, although it was probably deduced from music—a music, be it noted, that knew not polyphony or harmony, and formed its instruments to render single plump, almost fleshy, tones—seems to be the very mould for a sculpture that has this ideal. The worked stone is only a something in so far as it has considered limits and measured form; what it *is* is what it *has become* under the sculptor's chisel. Apart from this it is *chaos*, something not yet actualized, in fact for the time being a null. The same feeling transferred to the grander stage produces, as an opposite to the state of chaos, that of *cosmos*, which for the Classical soul implies a cleared-up situation of the external world, a harmonic order which includes each separate thing as a well-defined, comprehensible and present entity. *The Decline of the West* (New York, 1950), vol. 1, p. 63. See Wade *Letters*, p. 716, for Yeats's reference to Oswald Spengler.
69. See Alfred C. Foucher, *L'Art Greco—Buddique* 2. vols. (Paris, 1905–1918) and *Beginnings of Buddhist Art* (London, 1918). Foucher argues that the origin of the Buddha sculptures was classical Greece. They spread over the East later. Yeats shares the same theory in his 'Statues.' See also Ananda K. Coomaraswamy's article 'The Origin of the Buddha Image' *Art Bulletin* (June 1927) refuting this theory and his *Medieval Singhalese Art*, (New York, 1956), second edition, pp. 256–259, for a discussion of the influence of Greek art on Indian art.
70. 'The Statues.'
71. Ibid.
72. "Under Ben Bulben.'
73. Ibid.
74. *Autobiographies*, p. 83.

75. Ibid., p. 83.
76. *Essays and Introductions*, p. 522.
77. Ibid., p. 522.
78. Ibid., p. 523. Also cf. Yeats's poem "The Fisherman,' p. 145.
79. *Essays and Introductions*, p. 524.
80. *Letters of W.B. Yeats*, ed. Alan Wade (London, 1954), p. 608. Cited hereafter as *Letters*.
81. Ibid., p. 608.
82. Ibid., p. 609.
83. *Essays and Introductions*, p. 163.
84. Ibid., p. 164.
85. Ibid., p. 159.
86. Ibid., pp. 227–228.
87. W. H. Pater who was an important influence on Yeats deals with this aspect of style in his essay "On Style" in his *Appreciations* (London, 1911).
88. *Autobiographies*, p. 202.
89. Cf. *Essays and Introductions*, p. 476. "That shortest and the most comprehensive of *The Upanishads* examines the sacred syllables: 'the word *Aum* is the imperishable Spirit. This universe is the manifestation. The past, the present, the future, everything, is *Aum*, and whatever transcends this division of time, that too is *Aum*.'"
90. Ibid., p. 253.
91. 'A Coat.'
92. *Essays and Introductions*, p. 201.
93. Thomas Parkinson, *W.B. Yeats; the later poetry* (University of California Press, 1964).
94. Jon Stallworthy, *Between the lines; Yeats's poetry in the making* (Oxford, 1963).
95. 'Anashuya and Vijaya.'
96. 'The Sad Shepherd.'
97. 'The Indian to His Love.'
98. 'The Madness of King Goll.'
99. 'The Rose of Battle.'
100. 'Lapis Lazuli.'
101. 'A Bronze Head.'
102. 'Among School Children.'

## Chapter Two

1. Cf. "*Aum*, this syllable is all this. And explanation of that is the following. All this is the past, the present, and the future, all this is only the syllable *Aum*. And whatever else is beyond the threefold time that too is the only syllable *aum*." *Mandukya Upanishad, The Principal Upanishads*, trans. Radhakrishnan (London, 1969), p. 695. *The Upanishads* contain mystical speculations about the nature of speech sound. According to them the syllable *Aum* when repeatedly chanted can induce states of trance or supra-rational consciousness. Yeats was familiar with *The Upanishads* and translated them in collaboration with Swami Purohit Swami.
2. *Essays and Introductions*, p. 43.
3. Ibid., p. 22.
4. 'The Tower,' ll. 42–49. The chronology of Yeats's poems used in this study is based on G.B. Saul's *Prolegomena to the Study of Yeats's Poems* (Philadelphia, 1957).

5. Ibid., l. 92.
6. Ibid., ll. 55–57.
7. S.T. Coleridge, 'Kubla Khan,' ll. 46–48.
8. *Essays and Introductions*, p. 155.
9. Ibid., p. 497.
10. Ibid., pp. 189–190.
11. R. Krishnamurthy, *Anandavardhana's Dhvanyaloka* (Poona, 1955), p. 9.
12. Arthur Symons, *Symbolist Movement in Literature* (New York, 1958), p. 73.
13. *Essays and Introductions*, p. 193.
14. Arthur Symons, *The Symbolist Movement in Literature*, p. 73.
15. *Essays and Introductions*, p. 254.
16. Cf. Keats's use of "happy," "happiness," "truth," "beauty" in the *Odes*. These are key words and they link up the *Odes* in a sequence.
17. W. Empson analyses significant words within a single literary classic, for example, key words like "wit" in *The Essay on Criticism*, "All" in *Paradise Lost*, "Honest" in *Othello*, "Fool" in *King Lear* in *The Structure of Complex Words* (London, 1951). The analysis of complexity in Yeats's vocabulary attempted in this chapter covers his entire work taken as one continuous whole. Otherwise the phrase "complex words" is used in the same sense as by Empson.
18. Owen Barfield, *Poetic Diction* (New York, 1964).

## Chapter Three

1. For a discussion of the moon image in Yeats see Thoman F. Parkinson, *W.B. Yeats: The Later Poetry* (Univ. of California, 1964), p. 160.
2. 'The Wanderings of Oisin,' in the *Variorum Edition of the Poems of W.B. Yeats*, ed. Peter Allt and Russell K. Alspach (New York, 1966), p. 28.
3. 'On Woman.'
4. 'Phases of the Moon.'
5. 'Solomon and the Witch.'
6. Ibid.
7. 'Nineteen Hundred and Nineteen.'
8. *Variorum Edition of the Poems of W.B. Yeats*, p. 220.
9. 'Wanderings of Oisin,' Bk. I. ll. 50–51.
10. 'The Lover Pleads with His Friend for Old Friends.'
11. 'Who Goes with Fergus?'
12. 'The Two Trees.'
13. 'Ego Dominus Tuus.'
14. 'Cuchulain's Fight with the Sea.'
15. 'Parnell's Funeral.'
16. 'Why Should the Heart Take Fright?' *Variorum* ed. p. 781.
17. 'Why Does Your Heart Beat Thus?' *Variorum* ed. p. 785.
18. 'When Helen Lived.'
19. 'Meditations in Time of Civil War.'
20. Ibid.
21. 'The Tower,' ll. 148–152.
22. 'The Wanderings of Oisin,' Bk. I. l. 208.
23. 'Her Vision in the Wood.' l. 25.
24. 'Statistics.'
25. 'The Man Who Dreamed of Faeryland.'

26. 'Vacillation.'
27. 'To Some I Have Talked with by the Fire.'
28. 'The Phantom Ship,' l.21, *Variorum* ed.
29. 'Mosada,' 3.l.61, *Variorum* ed.
30. 'Ephemera,' *Variorum ed.*, 1.12b, p. 80.
31. 'To Some I Have Talked with by the Fire.'
32. 'Lapis Lazuli.'
33. 'A Cradle Song.'
34. 'The Host of the Air,' for a discussion of this poem see A.R. Grossman, *Poetic Knowledge in the Early Yeats* (University of Virginia Press, 1969), p. 164.
35. E. Engelberg, *The Vast Design* (University of Toronto Press, 1964), points out that Yeats may have been influenced by Arnold's essay 'On the Study of Celtic Literature' which stresses the Celtic origin of the word "gay," p. 170.
36. Cf. Keats, 'Ode to a Nightingale,' "Singest of summer in full-throated ease."
37. Cf. Keats, 'Endymion.'
38. Cf. 'Ode to a Nightingale,' "purple-stained mouth."
39. Cf. Keats, 'La Belle Dame Sans Merci,' "death-pale."

## Chapter 4

1. Edmund Spenser, 'An Hymne in Honour of Beautie,' 1. 132–134, *The Poetical Works of Edmund Spenser*, ed. J.C. Smith & E. De Selincourt (London, Oxford Univ. Press, 1937), p. 591.
2. *Letters*, p. 718.
3. Jon Stallworthy, *Vision and Revision in Yeats's Last Poems* (Oxford, 1969), p. 134.
4. *Autobiographies*, p. 175. For the influence of Irving's Hamlet as a fat prince cf. the following ll. in 'A Nativity'

    What brushes fly and moth aside?
    Irving and his plume of pride.

5. Edward Engelberg, *The Vast Design*, p. 181–187.
6. Walter Pater, *The Renaissance*, New York, 1959, p. 90.
7. Ibid., p. 90.
8. Ibid., p. 90.
9. Cf. Yeats's Interpretation and rendering of Pater's description of 'Mona Lisa' in his edition of *The Oxford Book of Modern Verse* (Oxford Univ. Press, 1936): "All these writers were, in the eye of the new generation, in so far as they were known, Victorian, and the new generation was in revolt. But one writer, almost unknown to the general public—I remember somebody saying at his death 'no newspaper has given him an obituary notice'—had its entire uncritical admiration, Walter Pater. That is why I begin this book with the famous passage from his essay on Leonardo da Vinci. Only by printing it in *vers libre* can one show its revolutionary importance. Pater was accustomed to give each sentence a separate page of manuscript, isolating and analyzing its rhythm. . . . I shall presently discuss the meaning of this passage which dominated a generation, a domination so great that all over Europe from that day to this men shrink from Leonardo's masterpiece as from an over-flattered woman. . . .

    I recall Pater's description of the Mona Lisa; had the individual soul of Da Vinci's sitter gone down with the pearl divers or trafficked for strange webs? or did Pater foreshadow a poetry, a philosophy, where the individual is nothing,

. . . human experience no longer shut into brief lives, cut off into this place and that place, . . ."

"She is older than the rocks among which she sits;
Like the Vampire,
She has been dead many times,
And learned the secrets of the grave;
And has been a diver in deep seas,
And keeps their fallen day about her;
And trafficked for strange webs with Eastern merchants;
And, as Leda,
Was the mother of Helen of Troy,
And, as St Anne,
Was the mother of Mary;
And all this has been to her but as the sound of lyres and flutes,
And lives
Only in the delicacy
With which it has moulded the changing lineaments,
And tinged the eyelids and the hands."

10. Walter Pater, *The Renaissance* (New York, 1959), p. 90.
11. *Essays and Introductions*, p. 227.
12. Ibid., p. 253.
13. T.R. Henn, *The Lonely Tower* (London, 1950), p. 113–120.
14. 'Two Songs from a Play,' see A.N. Jeffares, *Commentary on the Collected Poems of W.B. Yeats* (California, 1968), p. 290.
15. P.B. Shelley, 'Hellas,' chorus 1. 13–16, *The Poetical Works of Percy Bysshe Shelley* (Macmillan, London, 1900), p. 451.
16. *Essays and Introductions*, p. 369. "Hamlet's objection to the bare bodkin," establishes that the word "bodkin" in the poem is an allusion to Hamlet's "bodkin." Cf. Jon Stallworthy, *Vision and Revision in Yeats's Last Poems*, p. 65, and R.W. Desai, *Yeats's Shakespeare* (Northwestern Univ. Press, 1971), p. 264.
17. A. Norman Jeffares, *A commentary on the Collected Poems of W.B. Yeats*, p. 511.
18. See Harry Levin, *Question in Hamlet* (New York, 1959).
19. Stallworthy thinks this an echo of *Macbeth*, *Vision and Revision in Yeats's Last Poems* (Oxford, 1969), p. 65.
20. Ibid., p. 49.
21. Arthur Symons, *Symbolist Movement in Literature*, p. 105–106.
22. Cf.

Grant me an old man's frenzy,
Myself must I remake
Till I am Timon and Lear
Or that William Blake
Who beat upon the wall
Till Truth obeyed his call;
'An Acre of Grass.'

Cf.

All perform their tragic play,
There struts Hamlet, there is Lear,
That's Ophelia, that Cordelia;
Yet they, should the last scene be there,
The great stage curtain about to drop,
If worthy their prominent part in the play,
Do not break up their lines to weep.
They know Hamlet and Lear are gay;
Gaiety transfiguring all that dread.

All men have aimed at, found and lost;
Black out; Heaven blazing into the head:
Tragedy wrought to its uttermost.
Though Hamlet rambles and Lear rages,
And all the drop-scenes drop at once
Upon a hundred thousand stages,
It cannot grow by an inch or an ounce.
'Lapis Lazuli.'

23. See S.R. Swaminathan, 'Bhartrihari, Tagore and Yeats,' *Viswa Bharati Quarterly*, 1976.
24. 'A Prayer for My Daughter.'
25. *Essays and Introductions*, p. 193.
26. Ibid.
27. Arthur Symons, *The Symbolist Movement in Literature*, p. 70.
28. William Empson, *Seven Types of Ambiguity* (Connecticut, 1953), p. xi.

## Chapter Five

1. 'Under Ben Bulben.'
2. See Introduction to *Oxford Book of Modern Verse* (New York), 1936.
3. Cf. Yeats's recording of 'The Lake Isle of Innisfree.'
4. *Essays and Introductions*, p. 163.
5. *Letters*, p. 86.
6. Ibid., p. 325.
7. Ibid., p. 608.
8. Ibid., p. 709.
9. Ibid., p. 857.
10. Ibid., p. 278.
11. Ibid., p. 360.
12. Ibid., p. 441.
13. Ibid., p. 327.
14. Raymond Southall, *The Courtly Maker* (Oxford, 1964), p. 126.
15. *Essays and Introductions*, p. 159.
16. For a discussion of Yeats's poems written in the *ottava rima* see Robert Beum, *Poetic Art of W.B. Yeats* (Ungar, 1968), pp. 120–131, and Frank Kermode, *Romantic Image* (London, 1957), for Cowley's influence on Yeats. I have attempted a more detailed analysis of Yeats's eight-line stanza poems than Beum.
17. F.A.C. Wilson, *W.B. Yeats and Tradition* (London, 1958), p. 237.
18. *Letters*, p. 896.

## Chapter Six

1. Cf. Thomas Parkinson, *W.B. Yeats; The Later Poetry*, pp. 20–30. Cf. T.R. Henn, *The Lonely Tower*, pp. 35–50.
2. 'When You Are Old.'
3. 'Who Goes with Fergus?'
4. 'He Gives His Beloved Certain Rhymes.'
5. 'Broken Dreams.'
6. 'Sailing to Byzantium.'
7. 'The Tower.'
8. Cf. *Autobiographies*, "I still carried my green net but I began to play at being a

sage, a magician or a poet. I had many idols, and as I climbed along the narrow ledge I was now Manfred on his glacier, and now Prince Athanase with his solitary lamp, but I soon chose Alastor for my chief of men and longed to share his melancholy, and maybe at last to disappear from everybody's sight as he disappeared drifting in a boat along some slow-moving river between great trees," p. 41.

9. Cf. 'Lapis Lazuli.'
10. *Autobiographies*, p. 60.
11. Ibid., pp. 41–42.
12. *Letters*, p. 20.
13. Ibid., p. 122.
14. *Explorations*, ed. Mrs. W.B. Yeats (New York, 1962), p. 81.
15. Ibid., pp. 153–154.
16. Ibid., p. 155.
17. *Autobiographies*, pp. 57–58.
18. Ibid., p. 317–318.
19. *Explorations*, pp. 107–108.
20. See Robert Langbaum, *The Poetry of Experience* for a detailed discussion of the dramatic monologue, pp. 175–178. Definitions of the dramatic monologue vary. Some insist on poems like Browning's 'The Last Duchess' as being the type. See Ira Beth Sessions, *A Study of the Dramatic Monologue in America and Continental Literature* (Texas, 1933). This definition is rigid and narrow. Others like Langbaum make the definition wider to include poems like 'Lycidas,' The Song of Songs, and the Anglo Saxon 'Banished Wife's Complaint.' In this chapter the more flexible definition has been accepted. According to such a definition the dramatic monologue is a poem in which a speaker addresses one or more silent listeners.
21. Both John Unterecker, *A Reader's Guide to William Butler Yeats* (New York, 1959), pp. 92–93, and Allen R. Grossman, *Poetic Knowledge in the Early Yeats: A Study of the Wind Among the Reeds* (Virginia Univ. Press, 1969), pp. 20–21, have commented on this.
22. 'The Heart of the Woman.'
23. 'The Lover Mourns for the Loss of Love.'
24. 'He Gives His Beloved Certain Rhymes.'
25. Ibid.
26. 'The Lover Asks Forgiveness Because of His Many Moods.'
27. Ibid.
28. 'He Thinks of Those Who Have Spoken Evil of His Beloved.'
29. 'The Travail of Passion.'
30. 'The Arrow.'
31. 'Never Give All the Heart.'
32. 'O Do Not Love Too Long.'
33. 'King and No King.'
34. Max F. Schulz, *The Poetic Voices of Coleridge* (Wayne State University Press, Detroit, 1963), p. 82.

## Conclusion

1. Jon Stallworthy, *Vision and Revision* (Oxford, 1969), see also Thomas Parkinson, *W.B. Yeats: The Later Poetry*, pp. 73–113.

# A SELECT BIBLIOGRAPHY

I. Works of W.B. Yeats quoted, referred to, or consulted in this study.

*The Autobiography of William Butler Yeats*, New York, 1965.
*The Collected Poems*, Macmillan, Toronto, 1969.
*Essays and Introductions*, London, 1961.
*Explorations*, (ed.) Mrs. W. B. Yeats, New York, 1962.
*Letters*, (ed.) Alan Wade, London, 1954.
*Letters to Katharine Tynan*, New York, 1953.
*Letters to the New Island*, Cambridge, Mass., 1934.
*Letters on Poetry to Dorothy Wellesley*, London, 1940.
*Mythologies*, New York, 1959.
*Oxford Book of Modern Verse*, New York, 1936.
*Uncollected Prose*, (ed.) John P. Frayne, New York, 1970.
*The Variorum Edition of the Poems*, Allt and Alspach, Macmillan, 1957.
*A Vision*, Collier Books, 1969.
*W.B. Yeats and T. Sturge Moore: Their Correspondence 1901–1937*, (ed.) Ursula Bridge, New York, 1953.

II. Other works quoted or consulted in this study.

Bachchan, H.R., *W.B. Yeats and Occultism; a study of his works in relation to Indian lore, the Cabbala, Swedenborg, Boehme and Theosophy*, Delhi, 1965.
Barfield, Owen, *Poetic Diction*, New York, 1964.
Beum, Robert, *Poetic Art of W.B. Yeats*, Ungar, 1968.
Bradford, Curtis, *Yeats at Work*, Carbondale, Southern Illinois University Press, 1965.
———, *Yeats's 'Last Poems' Again*, Dolmen Press, 1966.
Coomaraswamy, Ananda K., *Medieval Sinhalese Art*, New York, 1956.
Davenport, A., "W.B. Yeats and *The Upanishads*," *Review of English Studies*, January, 1952.
Desai, R.W., *Yeats's Shakespeare*, Northwestern University Press, 1971.
Ellman, Richard, *Yeats: The Man and the Masks*, London, 1948.

Empson, William, *Seven Types of Ambiguity*, Conn., 1953.

Engelberg, E., *The Vast Design: Patterns in W.B. Yeats's Aesthetic*, University of Toronto Press, 1964.

Finneran, Richard J., *Editing Yeats's Poems*, St. Martin's Press, New York, 1983.

Grossman, A. R., *Poetic Knowledge in the Early Yeats; a study of the Wind Among the Reeds*, University Press of Virginia, 1969.

Henn, T. R., *The Lonely Tower; Studies in the Poetry of W.B. Yeats*, London, 1950.

Hone, J.M., *W.B. Yeats*, London, 1942.

Jeffares, A.N., *A Commentary on the Collected Poems of W.B. Yeats*, Stanford, 1968.

———, *W.B. Yeats, Man and Poet*, London, 1949.

Kermode, Frank, *Romantic Image*, London, 1957.

Krishnamurthy, R., *Anandavardhana's Dhvanyaloka*, Poona, 1955.

Langbaum, Robert, *The Poetry of Experience*, New York, 1957.

Levin, Harry, *Question in Hamlet*, New York, 1959.

Parkinson, Thomas, *W.B. Yeats; the later poetry*, University of California Press, 1964.

Parrish, S. Maxfield and Painter, J.A., *A Concordance to the Poems of W.B. Yeats*, Cornell University Press, 1963.

Radhakrishnan, S., *The Principal Upanishads*, trans., London, 1969.

Roe, F.R., (ed.) *Victorian Prose*, New York, 1947.

Saul, G.B., *Prolegomena to the Study of Yeats's Poems*, Philadelphia, 1957.

Schultz, Max F., *The Poetic Voices of Coleridge*, Detroit, 1963.

Stallworthy, Jon, *Between the Lines; Yeats's Poetry in the Making*, Oxford, 1963.

———, *Vision and Revision in Yeats's Last Poems*, Oxford, 1969.

Swami, Purohit, and Yeats, W.B., (ed.) *The Ten Principal Upanishads*, London, 1970.

Symons, Arthur, *Symbolist Movement in Literature*, New York, 1958.

Southall, Raymond, *The Courtly Maker*, Oxford, 1964.

Ure, Peter, '"The Statues" A note on the meaning of Yeats's poem,' *Review of English Studies*, July, 1949.

———, *Towards a Mythology*, London, 1946.

Unterecker, John, *A Reader's guide to W.B. Yeats*, New York, 1959.

# INDEX